Child of the

Accompany a Missionary's Kid whose memories of life begin far from any civilization amongst the Australian Aborigines, and track her subsequent lifelong adventures and struggles of trying to fit into "normal" society.

Outback

childoftheoutback@juno.com

Marilyn Stewart

*John —
Numbers 6:24-26
Psalm 139
Blessings!
M Stewart
(Karlkurla)*

Cover art by Cathi A. Wong
E-mail: caw004@aol.com

Copyright © 2000 by Marilyn Stewart

All rights reserved. No part of this book shall be reproduced or transmitted in any form or by any means, electronic, mechanical, magnetic, photographic including photocopying, recording or by any information storage and retrieval system, without prior written permission of the publisher. No patent liability is assumed with respect to the use of the information contained herein. Although every precaution has been taken in the preparation of this book, the publisher and author assume no responsibility for errors or omissions. Neither is any liability assumed for damages resulting from the use of the information contained herein.

ISBN 0-7414-0303-X

Published by:

Infinity Publishing.com
519 West Lancaster Avenue
Haverford, PA 19041-1413
Info@buybooksontheweb.com
www.buybooksontheweb.com
Toll-free (877) BUY BOOK
Local Phone (610) 520-2500
Fax (610) 519-0261

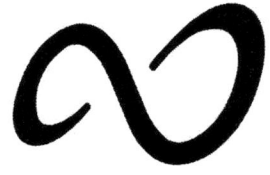

Printed in the United States of America
Printed on Recycled Paper
Published December-2000

This book is dedicated to JOHN in appreciation of his wit, commitment, and love.

A special Thanks to:

My parents: Bob and Ethel Stewart who not only gave me life and strove to do what they thought was best for me, but also for their constant prayers.

John and Betty Thompson who in 1957 opened not only their home, but also their hearts to me - an unknown Child from the Australian Outback.

Father Ed and Hazel Edstrom, yes, you too Linda, for welcoming me and making me "family," when I again needed a safe haven in 1962.

Darlene, Dale, and Stephen, just for being my beloved sister and brothers.

And to the following who after reading my manuscript pushed and encouraged me to publish - Jaye, John & Betty, Keith, Guy & Marie, and Kelly.

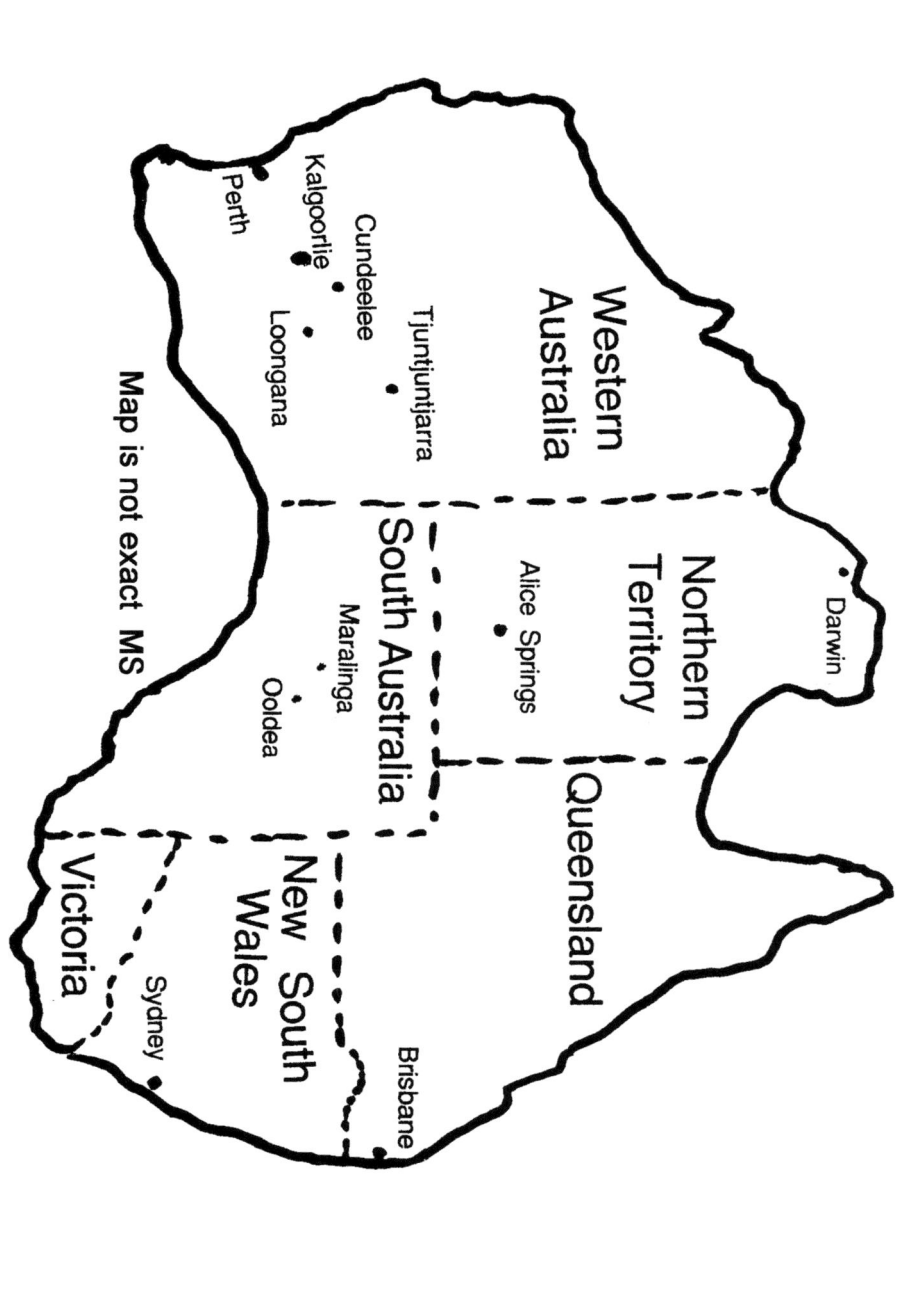

A fascinating autobiography written with rare transparency!
Guy of Mesa, AZ.

This is a magnificent story of a person who had every reason to shrivel up and die, but who has retained her Faith and trust. Her life indeed has been an unusual adventure.
John & Betty of Pahrump, NV.

I found it a "page turner!" and was up until 1:00 a.m. reading -- couldn't put it down. Kelly of Phoenix, AZ.

Accompany a Missionary's Kid who experiences life as an Aborigine playmate, sexually abused child, "shipped-out" student, and finally a mature Christian. Eyes-glued reading. Jaye of Mesa, AZ.

Finished your excellent book in one sitting. It's a smashing good story. I give it two thumbs up! Keith of Elk Grove, CA.

This is a riveting, straightforward account of a survivor. A real eye-opener! Be prepared to pick it up for a second reading. Should be required reading for every missionary candidate.
Marie of Mesa, AZ.

Little Karlkurla shares with us her Heart, Soul and Faith.
Rosalie of Mesa, AZ.

A wonderfully sensitive and deeply touching true story of a seemingly disadvantaged child growing into a woman of God's destiny. Richard & Diane of Albuquerque, NM.

This true autobiographical account is as much a page-turner as the best seller fiction book I read last week. Michelle Mgr. Family Christian Store of Olympia, WA.

Table of Contents

Introduction
Background & Book

<u>Section One</u> is about growing up in the real Outback of Western Australia among the Aborigines.

Tide & Trees 1
Pumpkin & Pie 5
Gums & Galah 9
Names & Nyndi 13
Culture & Cundeelee 17
Family & Feet 25
Butter & Bardi 29
Braids & Birds 33
Words & Wangatha 37
Tires & Tucker 41
Doctor & Doll 47
Poems & Punishment 53
Homes & Heaven 59
Trousers & Truth 63
Christmas & Creek 69

Section Two deals with culture shock, constant fear due to sexual abuse, of foster homes, boarding school and separation from family.

Departure & Devils 81
Rain & Relatives 91
Classes & Cold 95
Deserted & Dorm 101
Announcement & Adopted 105
Cage & Cars 109
Recess & Reading 113
Birthday & Boys 117
Machines & Music 121
Rules & Roommates 125
Peeling & Praises 133
Farms & Felines 135
Varnish & Violence 139
Banff & Bears 143
Parents & Promises 147

Section Three deals with continuing emotional problems, moving to the USA, college, marriage, returning to visit the Outback, and the two-way gift of blessing.

Seattle & Spelling 153
Summer & Stuck 157
Edstroms & Excursions 161
Stephen & Speech 167
College & Caring 171
Motorola & Marriage 177
Birth & Burial 185
Life & Longings 193
Return & Release 201
Flying & Firmament 209
Pomeranians & Personalities 215
Lax & Lost 219
Blessed & Blessing 225

Epilogue 231

Glossary 233

Introduction:

I had no intention of ever writing or having a story written about my life until October 20, 1997. I had considered what had happened to be not only private, but also too painful to share with anyone. I had to deal with or work though the hurts of my past before I could write them down and finally begin the healing process. I had just returned from a ladies retreat in which the theme had been "Choose Joy." The topic had started me reflecting on choices - those others had made that almost destroyed my life, to ones I have made. Each day I have to make a choice not to live in my past, but to accept it as past and move into the future with renewed hope and trust in a God who loves me.

I had come back from the retreat with a cough, sore throat, and some time on my hands. Monday morning came, and it was as if it was time for this book of remembrances to materialize. I walked into our computer room, sat down, placed my fingers on the keyboard and started to type. It took two days before my husband came in and said, "what are you doing?" I had never spent so much time at the computer without papers strewn around me, and it was obvious I had none. I said "guess," to which he jokingly replied, "I suppose you'll tell me you are writing a book."

This true story of my life with its many ups and downs is seen through my perspective and memories of happenings.

Background & Book

My name is Karlkurla, which in the Wangatha dialect of the Western Australian Aborigine means "Wild Pear." I am a little ahead of my story which really started for me, in the year 1938 when Robert Stanley Stewart at twenty, took Ethel Francis Hollinger age seventeen, to be his bride.

In 1944 at West Seattle General Hospital, I, Marilyn Stewart, was the third child to survive in this family. According to my mother, because I was so quiet, I was allowed to stay with her in church meetings and classes (to the envy of other mothers) from the time I was three weeks old. When my older brother Dale was born the doctors did not believe that either my mother or brother would survive. My father being informed of this by the doctor, went out, and prayed to God, although he was not a praying, nor a religious man, saying he would serve Him, if God brought them both through this safely. When his prayers were answered with the safe arrival of the baby and the quick recovery of his wife he remembered his promise. He started attending church with his wife and two young children. It was a small Christian and Missionary Alliance church, where they taught the scriptures starting with "ye must be born again." Now he was a "good moral man and loving husband" and struggled with the fact that according to the scriptures these good qualities would not get him into Heaven. One day as he read the Bible he was struck by the fact that God loved him so very much that He had sent Jesus to die for his sins, and that it was a free gift if he would only accept it. Mum had done this as a young child in Sunday school and had been praying for her beloved husband. He was a shy, quiet fellow; however, after accepting God's free gift he suddenly wanted to share this good news with others. He little dreamed what this decision would cost him and his family, nor the joy and thanks he'd receive from hundreds of people with whom he eventually shared this good news.

Although he had a good job working at Elliot Bay Mill Company, and now had three children, his pastor encouraged him to go to Bible College, and not just any Bible College, but one in cold Alberta, Canada.

In 1946, Dad quit his job at Elliott Bay Mill Company, packed up his family with their few possessions, but that is another story, and one which my sister Darlene is writing in great detail.

I hope you will enjoy my real life true story -

"Child of the Outback."

Australia

An Outback Child at heart am I,
In culture and language until I die.

If we confess our sins, He is faithful and just to forgive us our sins and to cleanse us from all unrighteousness.   1 John 1:9

Tide & Trees

Despite noise being generated by four engines, the wind, rain, and our being wrapped up in blankets we heard the following at almost the same instant. The pilot's voice over the intercom saying, "if anyone knows how to pray I suggest you do it now," and treetops hitting the under carriage of the airplane in which we were passengers.

My memories of events and happenings only go back as far as when I was five and a half years old – everything before that is a blank. Our family was in a large (for that era) thirty-six-passenger airplane. I was cold and scared. It was February of 1950, and we were enroute to Australia. We had left from Vancouver, flown for eight hours to Hawaii where we had a thirty-six hour layover before heading on towards Fiji. In Hawaii we had enjoyed having a day to start adjusting to the warmer weather we would soon feel. At the edge of the beach coconut trees grew, and a man was climbing the trees throwing the huge "nuts" to the ground for the tourists. I had been fascinated at the speed and manner in which he climbed the trees, for he barely used hands, and his feet were bare. Up until this time I had not seen an adult outside the house without shoes on their feet. I made sure to be out of the way when he threw the coconuts down onto the sand near the base of the tree. I was sure his feet must hurt, but they looked okay when he came over to show us where to make holes to allow us to drink the milk straight from the freshly picked coconut.

Having just come from winter weather, and heading for a dry desert, we didn't have any swim suits in our luggage. Therefore I was allowed to tuck the bottom of my dress up into the elastic of my panties, so I could play in the sand and walk at the edge of the ocean. I became tired of playing in the sand and went down into the water just to wash the sand off of my hands. The next thing I remember was how my feet felt as if they were being sucked right out from under me. I tried to struggle back to shore, but could only move enough to angle my head backwards keeping it above the water. I was flaying at the water with one hand while desperately waving the other in hopes that someone would see it. The water rose steadily and all too quickly was over my mouth and splashing into my nose. Just as my feet lifted from the sand and I started to float out to sea I felt a hand grab a hold of mine, and pull me back. It was my brother Dale who had quietly come to my rescue. No one else saw what nearly happened to me, or that he had just saved my life from the scary sucking ocean current. Not wanting to draw attention to ourselves or get in trouble, this drama remained a secret between us and yet it typified the way my older brother tried to watch out for me.

The next day we continued our journey toward Australia. Leaving Hawaii we flew for six long, strapped down, bouncing hours before finally descending to a runway in the Canton Islands. The pilot decided we would stay put overnight due to a strong storm, which was building rapidly, but we were to be ready to push on to Fiji early the next day. When we finally arrived in Fiji we would have been very happy to stay and wait for better weather for our flight to Sydney, for the storm was now classified as a tropical hurricane.

However, the pilot had the final say and decided we would push on regardless of the strong winds and heavy rains we were experiencing. We tensed as we looked out the plane's small rain battered windows and raced down the runway trying to generate enough speed in order to lift off of the tarmac. Before reaching the end of the runway there was a sudden and drastic decrease in the noise and vibration of the plane and we slowed to a crawl. As our plane turned and slowly headed back towards the terminal, we breathed a sigh of relief, but then we turned yet again, and quickly realized we were lining up for another try at taking off. The pilot had his heart set on trying to fly out right now rather than be grounded for several days due to the storm. Despite noise being generated by four engines, the wind, rain, and our being wrapped up in blankets, we heard the following at almost the same instant. The pilots voice over the intercom saying, "if anyone knows how to pray I suggest you do it now," and treetops hitting the under carriage of the airplane in which we were passengers. It was at this point that another miracle in our journey occurred. As we prayed the plane lifted, and not only rose enough to clear the trees, but also to keep climbing high enough to again be bouncing in and out above the clouds. We said a heartfelt "Thank You, Jesus," for His protection and reassurance that He really did want all of us in the Outback of Australia!

I was even grateful when they provided and reprovided those little brown sacks (except in my thinking they were white in color) to lose my stomach contents into as we climbed and dropped for the next five hours on the last leg of our journey to Australia. I have been an extremely nervous flyer ever since, preferring to keep my feet on solid ground. As we progress with my story you'll see that I've had to deal with the stress of floating through the sky, more often than I have wished, and so far, much to my delight, have lived to tell about it!

Pumpkin & Pie

On our arrival in Australia things were not as ready for us at the mission station in the Outback of Australia as my folks had been led to believe. In those days mail took anywhere from two to even four months to travel from Australia to the USA. The mission board had posted a letter telling us to delay our journey; however, never having received it, we arrived unexpectedly "on their doorstep." It had been with the president of the school's blessing (due to Dad's age) that we had left four months before Dad was to graduate from Bible College. The need for him in the Outback of Australia had been stressed as urgent, and now the mission was in the process of deciding where to start a new work, since the other one had fallen through. We ended up staying for about two months in Sydney.

After the Second World War many American servicemen had taken Aussie women home to America with them, and here we were - Americans, and coming to work as missionaries amongst their Aborigines! The majority of Australians did not welcome our family with open arms, but we children were treated with great kindness and each of us was given a couple of nice toys not only just to play with, but also to keep.

Again it was time to move on, only this time it meant crossing Australia by train, which was anything but dull, and took a week to accomplish. Each time we entered a new province (state), we had to change to a completely new train due to the rail gauge being a different width. Our changes usually occurred in the middle of the night, which meant all of the luggage, boxes, etc. we had brought with us had to be moved from one train to the next. With not a lot of time in which to make the transfer each one of us carried as much as we could the first time over; then our job was to stay put, while Dad raced back and forth over tracks and between the trains. No one offered to help him and each time he worried he'd not get everything or the new train would leave while he was still at the old one getting our stuff. A couple of times during the trip we suddenly woke up due to the lack of motion, and grabbed for our clothes only to learn the train had a "hot box" and we could go back to sleep.

It was after this cross-country trip that a strange split up of our family occurred and lasted for several very confusing and strange months for us kids. The location chosen by the mission board for the new mission station was in a remote area of Western Australia. There was nothing at this location but dirt and trees; therefore, Dad and another missionary, a Mr. Soper, went ahead to build a place for us to live. By now it was known Mum was once again pregnant, and because of her previous medical history the doctor thought it best for her to stay at or near the hospital in Kalgoorlie, until after the baby was born. I understood Dad going out to Cundeelee, but I never understood why we didn't at least live in the same town as our Mum even if we couldn't live in the same house with her. My sister Darlene, brother Dale and I were left to live with an unknown middle-aged spinster lady in a place called Loongana. The house was right next to the railroad and located on the Nullabor Plain - a desolate desert area that encompasses hundreds of miles in Western Australia. It was aptly named Nullabor (meaning no trees) for we could look in any direction and because of the flat land, all we could see was dirt and small rocks. It felt very hot, but was actually only a mild foretaste of the heat we'd feel in the middle of summer. When Dad left us there he assigned Darlene the job of looking out for us since she was the oldest. At eleven it was a big responsibility and one she struggled with emotionally as she tried to fulfill it to the best of her ability. Home for the next three or so months was right next to the railway siding (line), where other than cattle yards, which were empty most of the time, and a few homes, there was nothing and lots of it.

We experienced our first pangs of lost security and the pain of separation from our parents. Little did we know how many of these separations would take place in our future, and that eventually they would last for years. This was only the first tiny step in a series that started preparing me for some tough years in my future. It was the first of many homes I would live in far from loving natural parents. Eventually it would include being cut off from the Aborigine people and customs I thought were my own, as well as from my sister, and brothers.

I know now that the spinster lady we were staying with tried hard to please three foreign children who were sorely missing their mum and dad. She was not used to dealing with children at all, had no idea of what to make of us, or even how much or what foods we were used to eating.

While Mum had always told us that we had to take and eat a little of everything, even if we didn't care for it, this lady believed in filling our plates herself, and then we had to sit at the table until we had cleaned our plate. She must have overheard us talking about pumpkin pie, because one day she told us she would make us a pumpkin pie, if we were good. In spite of the fact that she did not have a recipe, had never even seen or tasted a pumpkin pie, she gave it a go. There weren't any pumpkins available; however, she did manage to find a stringy old squash. She proceeded to mash it up a bit, add a couple of spices, put it in the oven, and when it was sort of cooked but still a little runny, she decided it was done and ready to be eaten.

It was always an interesting meal we sat down to, but that night when she told us what it was, we looked at it in disbelief, and were rather vocal in stating that pumpkin pie it was Not. Not having won the favor she desired, and having me upchuck it back onto the plate after one bite, she returned with a clean plate and even more food, especially the "pumpkin pie," saying each of us would sit there until we had cleaned our plates. We had not been thrilled with "Thank you Lord for this food to eat," when we started the meal, and that night time seemed to pass so very slowly as I tried to choke down the food on my plate. I was so very thankful that Australians automatically put bread on the table at meal times, and although she had withheld it at first finally brought some to the table. This was the first time that I consciously realized if I ate enough bread with my meal I could get any food down almost untasted. Darlene got her "pie" down first and was able to leave the table, but I had to wait until the bread arrived before I could get my supper down. I took a tiny bit of "pie" then stuffed my mouth full of bread, and after three slices of well buttered bread the food was down and I was near bursting. I have always been one to try to do what I was told, not rock the boat, work at pleasing everyone, hear and see everything taking place near me, while at the same time endeavoring to remain almost invisible.

Dale waited her out past his bedtime, and would not lower himself to my method of using the bread to get it down. He ended up going to bed somewhat hungry, but figured he had won the silent war going on regarding eating all of his supper, and went to bed happy in spite of the warning "I'm going to tell your Dad" hanging over his head.

Darlene could usually be found working alone in the house going over and over her schoolwork. Dale and I on the other hand had great fun out on the desert turning over rocks and twigs to see what would be hiding underneath. We found the most amazing creatures such as centipedes, lizards, scorpions, and spiders as well as all kinds of bugs hiding in any available shade. Fortunately for us, most of the time they were far more interested in finding more shade than in making the effort to attack us.

Gums & G...

After being separated from our... ...day Dad arrived seemingly out of... ...home. I felt such relief to finally... ...and that we were all going to g... ...home was to be at Cundeelee... ...like an Indian reservation, ex... ...The mission operated under... ...Aborigines Evangelical Mis... ...the years many individua... ...church related) came to... ...period of time or until a r... ...was about five hundred... ...located on the West Co... ...road miles from the very nearest... ...mileage of one hundred sixty five m... ...rough and barely discernible trail of twenty-six miles that headed north from the nearest transline (railroad). A dot on the map signifying a "town" called Zanthus, in reality was not a town at all. Six or so houses used by railway personnel while maintaining the rails, and a small hut with a big sounding name of "The Depot," was all that was there. It was in front of "the depot" that the "goods" train stopped once a week to drop off our mail, once-in-a-while a passenger, and most important of all - our food supplies. At the same time outgoing mail was picked up along with the food order for the following week.

Our arrival at Cundeelee is etched like a photo in my mind comprised of mostly black and white images, for it took place in the evening long after the sun had set. The world around us was bathed in silence broken only by the muffled sound of our engine. We crept slowly yet ever onward, through sandy areas, over rocks, around and through brush. Dad kept assuring us we were going in the right direction in spite of it being so dark and visibility limited to only what our truck headlights illuminated. The stars seemed so huge, bright, and to cover the entire sky. It felt as if they were pressing downward yet hung just barely out of reach. I wondered if I was going to be crushed by their power yet was awed with their majestic brilliance and multitude. As the full moon made its appearance the stars sort of faded just a little in the added light. As the moon continued to rise, we could finally pick out not only the trees, and where best to drive, but also the shapes of kangaroos feeding in the shadows. In spite of these diversions, the miles seemed endless as we swayed and bounced on hard cold seats. For the next six years this would be the one and only road leading to or from my home to any spot of civilization.

In time the tiny glow in the distance grew and vague shapes were visible, which eventually turned into discernible real live Aborigines waving burning sticks. At about the same time the unknown roar-like noise turned into a distinct and understandable chant. Our arrival at Cundeelee was croaked in an unusual welcome as well – one by frogs, thanks to a recent rain. As the truck took the final last small rise and stopped, the fire stick waving, (to keep away the evil spirits) Aborigines started chanting "Upurl Upurlila, Cundeelee." The Aborigines had stayed up at the mission (about a mile from their camp) this particular night, just to welcome Dad's children to their new home. It was a truly amazing thing for them to do for these people were ruled by fear and were usually too afraid to go anywhere after dark because of evil spirits. By the time we arrived I was not only exhausted from traveling, but long overdue on sleep so was put straight to bed. It was the next morning that I met my baby brother Stephen, found out that we lived in a tent, had an out house out back, no running water or electricity, and that my future playmates spoke a different language.

The Aborigines accepted me into their tribe right from the start, for as a child I posed no threat to them. I never thought of myself as being "white" or in any way different from them. They let me share their food and quietly taught me their ways. My feet quickly outgrew my sandals and since there were no nearby stores to obtain new footwear, I was allowed to run barefoot just like the Aborigines for the next six years. I proceeded to do what I had always done, which was to watch, listen, learn, and imitate. In very short order I was on my way to becoming a true Child of the Outback in every way, be it cultural, language, play, or the way in which I thought and looked at life. Cundeelee was close to but not quite in the area referred to on the map as the Nullabor Plain. We sat at the top of a small rocky hill, which gave us a great, and to me a seemingly endless, wonderful view of a valley populated by trees. The vegetation around my new home was varied and interesting with red dirt, and spinifex, (similar to a cactus with three inch long spines, but in circular clumps on the ground) as well as many varieties of shrubs and trees. My favorite was the elegant red gray Eucalyptus trees, which Mum called the ghostly gums. I enjoyed watching the many different types of birds darting in and out of the trees, especially during the "wet" season. There were small finches with yellow beaks and bright splashes of color on their bodies, brilliantly colored lorikeets, birds that made their nest underground, the budgerigars in yellow and green, and of course the infamous Galah to name a few. The Galah is a type of cockatoo, which is stunningly pink on its front as well as under its wings, with the rest of its body a soft gray color. To refer to someone as a "Galah" was not a compliment, since the bird was known as lacking in good sense. When something was thrown into the air at or near the bird, it would fly towards the object to check it out, often getting hit in the process. Thus its curiosity or stupidity would often be the cause of its own death.

The sunsets were truly awesome and crowned this special quiet place of elegant trees, Aborigines, and kangaroos as home. Besides my home of the brush-covered tent, there was NO other building, store, or shop, there was very little water, lots of flies, Aborigines, red dirt, and strange looking animals. We were camping seven days a week, with only a kerosene lantern and a primus stove. I learned very quickly that all water had to be boiled and not even as little as a mouthful was ever to be tossed out or wasted. I understood that Mum and Dad were very busy for all day long I saw them helping people in any way they could; be it emotionally, medically or physically. I dimly realized they were also dealing every day with the problems of our health and survival. Since they were now always nearby I was content all was well with my world and basically ran "wild."

I tried very hard to do nothing to cause them any problems, which to me meant keeping out of the way as much as possible, for a tent was small for a family of six. I therefore, reveled in absorbing the culture and language of the Aborigines, until I felt as if I was one of them and soon no longer thought first in English.

The purchase and arrival of a short wave radio gave us a link to the "outside" world, but it really did not change anything for me. Although I was not allowed to touch it I often sat near Dad to watch and listen as he operated this amazing box. This "box" with the "call name" of 9EK was mainly used to check in and talk to the Flying doctor for advice or in an emergency. It was also the only way to send or receive important messages, or once-in-a-while listen in to the School of the Air broadcast. The radio usually worked well with good reception from nine in the morning until about four in the afternoon; however, after that time there was no sending or receiving any messages regardless of how important or urgent. From four in the afternoon on - all that could be heard through the headset was ear-splitting STATIC.

Names & Nyndi

Dad and Mr. Sopher were kept busy getting the station up and running, filling out all of the paper work required by both the government and the mission board, and putting together a tank out of corrugated iron to catch rainwater. The two men were also endeavoring to meet the medical, physical, and spiritual needs of all living at or near the station, learning a new language, as well as trying to find time for family.

The population at Cundeelee fluctuated between fifty and two hundred and fifty Aborigines depending on how many went "walkabout" at the same time. All day long curious people watched to see how, what, and why these strange people did things, and in turn try to figure out (never asking of course) how it would affect them.

The Australian Government had found it very hard to figure out how many Aborigines lived in this or any area of the Outback, and asked the missionaries' help in a couple ways. The government representatives said that the government would supply tea, sugar, flour, and chewing tobacco for the Aborigines, but the missionaries would be the ones responsible for distributing it correctly. The supplies would be referred to as rations. Precise records were to be kept as to which Aboriginal families at Cundeelee received the weekly rations. In this way the government would not have to "waste" an official "way out in the bush." Instead a man would be sent out periodically to check on the books, people, and the mission in general.

Another requirement made was to give or make sure that every Aboriginal that came to the station had an English name. They meant first and last, which meant figuring out who was related to whom. This took a lot of time, and before the task was completed several mix-ups occurred. It took a couple of years before all of the last names were finally correct. Family groups were not readily identifiable by outsiders; for one thing - the Aborigines did not build a "western style" type home. When on the move their home could simply be a scooped out hollow, or the shade of a large tree; however, if they were staying for a while then a lean-to of poles and brush was constructed and served as home until it was time to move on.

The men and teenage boys were often off on their own for special rites, or to hunt for meat for the tribe; therefore, they were not seen every day. The children and women hunted each day in small groups for anything edible; ranging from ants, eggs and grubs, to berries, birds, lizards, and snakes.

One day there could be two hundred Aborigines in camp and the next only thirty as most had left to go "walkabout." When returning from a trip they might be with another family group they claimed was kin, but was it blood kin or tribal kin – it had to be sorted out afresh – all in a strange language. The government had wanted each Aborigine that came to the station to be given an English name, for ease in record keeping, and as a sort of census taking. Dad soon found an even better reason for giving each person an English name; however, before understanding came, death made a visit to our compound. We found out very quickly after the death, that it was now a taboo to ever say the dead person's Wangkai name again under any circumstance. Their English name was okay to say, because to them it didn't have any significance or mean anything; whereas, their Wangkai name was their spirit, and must not be tampered with, especially after death. A child was never named at birth, due in part to the high mortality rate, but rather earned their name later in life due to a characteristic, habit or peculiarity of theirs, which described them in a way everyone recognized as an apt description of them.

In the following paragraphs I share a few examples of the endless variety of possible names, and the ways in which a few of them were "earned."

One of my little playmates loved to play with spiders. She was constantly catching them (remember they had no toys), and had even been known to pull off a leg to see if it could still walk. She was not partial to any special kind of spider. Over the years as she continued this behavior they named her Impu, which in the Wangatha language means spider without specifying the type.

As a youngster Mum had struggled to hear what was going on around her. Even sitting in the front row at school had not helped her very much for there was something wrong with her eardrums or lack of eardrums. It was years after I was gone from home that

Mum had an operation, which gave her the ability to hear normal conversations. In the meantime even with a hearing aid, although out in the bush at least half of the time she didn't have batteries for it, she could rarely hear all of what was being said. The people were very quick to pick up on her inability to hear and so named her Pina Loongoo. The name my Mum was given meant, "ear that is deaf, blocked, or cannot hear."

My baby brother, Stephen, having arrived at Cundeelee shortly after his birth was a novelty. The Aborigine women loved to carry him around. As a result of daily hearing his many baby sitters talking the first word Stephen spoke was in Wangatha, and the word was "nyndi." Because the Aborigines were so tickled by the fact that he had spoken their language before he spoke any English, it was decided that Nyndi would become his Wangkai name. It was early to name a child, but it was significant since it did not mean "mummy" nor did it relate to a person, for the basic meaning of the word was "to know or to understand." Depending on the inflection or tone used the one word "nyndi" could be used to ask a person if they understood what was going on, or to answer a question that I understood what had been said. Interestingly enough Stephen is the only one of us children "to know" or live almost his entire life in the Outback with the Aborigines.

Now my older brother Dale liked to climb trees as most boys do, and he particularly liked the trees with berries in them. One certain tree which Dale enjoyed climbing was known especially for a peculiarity that afflicted most of it's berries, because after one had taken a bite into it ... I'll just say that the name in English was almost always descriptively correct, and means "berry-with-a-half-a-worm-inside" or Tjaulyka Warulyka. Since most of the Aborigines in our area of the Outback were short in stature, Dale in time was also given a second "first" name, which was a rare occurrence in their culture. The second name was given because of his continued growth in height and his resulting long neck. To them he was beginning to rival the longest necked, tallest and fastest bird that was common in our outback area. His second name was the description of an emu - long neck.

A Karlkurla or wild pear was more like a vegetable than a fruit, was moist inside, but not juicy, and had several what I'd call layers to it. It had a smooth green colored outer skin, grew to be about six inches long and two inches in width. Wild pears could usually be spotted hanging in clusters of two or three dangling from a thin vine, high in a bush or a dead tree. If it had been hanging on the vine for a long time, I preferred it cooked slowly in the ashes of a fire before eating it; however, if it was young and tender I loved to eat it raw. In the morning after locating my wild pear snack of the day, I'd slowly start to eat it starting at one end and by evening I was at the other end. Inside the pear the first layer was similar in texture, taste and color to the inside rind of an Orange. The next layer consisted of long white silky fibers, which could be sucked on for moisture, and the center was made up of edible seeds. The seeds reflected the age of the pear by their color and also by their flavor since the sweet tasting green-yellow seeds turned yellow and became quite bitter as the plant aged. When the Karlkurla were in season I was adept at finding them, and quickly learned how to get one down without damage to the vine. During its growing season it was a rare day that I couldn't be spotted carrying a half eaten one in my hand.

Because of my fondness for them as well as the habit I had of carrying one with me to snack on throughout the day I was given the name Wild Pear or Karlkurla.

Culture & Cundeelee

The entire first section of this book takes place in the 1950s when humane treatment of the Australian Aborigines was just starting to become a real talked about issue. To many Australians at this time in history, the Aborigines were considered to be subhuman and pests. Sentiment in the country ranged from embarrassment, resentment and fear concerning them, to shame over their treatment and a willingness to work for change on their behalf.

The Aborigines of Western Australia were animistic in religion, and nomadic in order to stay alive in a hostile desert type of environment. They were dark skinned with wide flat noses, and eyes that God set far enough back under the eyebrow so as to be shaded from the sun. They lived for the most part in the desert area of the Outback, or the interior (middle section) of Australia.

They traveled very lightly in regards to possessions and very fast in terms of walking, always on the trail of food and water. Following their well-known routes they would travel from one rock hole that hopefully had caught some water, on to the next. Each time they would try to take the route they remembered as having the most food available and the shortest distance to walk to get a drink of water. Although they took many routes and covered a lot of territory, they considered the center of their homeland to be a place called Tjuntjuntjara. This "place" was located about 400 miles inland and east of Kalgoorlie. When they traveled it was usually with less than forty people in any one group. More often than not it was only a couple of small families together numbering around ten to fifteen in all. Every few years at a prearranged time and place hundreds of Aborigines would gather together, even for a brief period of time when food was scarce. There would be a "sing," maybe a marriage, and always the swapping of stories. It wasn't as if the groups were completely isolated from each other, for they not only "read" where people were going, they knew how many, if anyone was ill, and even left special messages for each other at route crossings. Most lived so far in the interior that they never crossed paths with any "civilization" during their entire lives, which would include seeing a person of another race, a vehicle, or even for example, anything made out of glass, plastic or paper. Their routes covered a lot of area and could take them from Cundeelee and Tjuntjuntjara over as far as Maralinga near Ooldea in South Australia. It was around this last area where they roamed so innocent and freely that the government was testing all of its rockets and weapons of war.

As the years passed and the Aborigines came to respect and trust the missionaries, and my parents in particular, they came to Dad asking for his help. They wished for either Dad to go into the interior and find their people, with their help of course, and bring them out to Cundeelee or for the government to stop the testing. Dad talked to many in government positions mostly to no avail, for most said there were no people in the area and others did not care. It was only after much badgering, and a trip into the interior that met with success in finding people there that things began to change. Some men from the government came to the missionaries at Cundeelee with a new request. "Take some of us back into the interior and prove to us there really are Aborigines living in this inhospitable desert area where our weapons of war are being tested."

The exciting trip into the vast interior, which took months to plan and weeks to accomplish, was finally achieved by Dad, several Aboriginal guides and a couple of government men.

My sister writes about this exciting chapter in Dad's life in great detail in her book.

When Aborigines saw "white" people for the first time, they immediately thought of ghosts and evil spirits. Strange things draped or hid the body of these colorless and maybe bloodless beings.

At one such first encounter, a brave young boy, ran up to Dad, grabbed his hand and bit it hard enough to draw blood. His bravery had proved to all it was not a ghost, but a human standing before them speaking albeit haltingly in their dialect.

The most elaborate home they ever constructed was only a half shelter or leanto using a few poles or limbs from dead trees, and then weaving small live bushes through the framework.

Their home gave very little protection from the elements, but they were built facing the direction that would give them most protection from the sun and the wind. These simple and quick to make homes were easy to build as well as to leave. For sanitary reasons, when they were staying in the same area for an extended period of time, they would move their camp about once a month. All they needed to do to move was for the men to pick up their spear, spear thrower, shield, and boomerang, and the women to pick up their wooden bowl, and special digging tool. They could be off at a moment's notice. After being at Cundeelee for a while, a couple of blankets, and a billy tin to hold food, brew tea or carry precious water, would be added to their moving list. When someone died, the whole tribe immediately moved to a new location, and after several years the elements would erase the previous "camp."

The only items they made were used primarily for hunting, light to carry, and usually created out of mulga, which was a hard wood. Using a fire, wood and stones (later a knife or tomahawk), each man would fashion his own weapons. I never remember being afraid of these stone-age people who could look so very ferocious. The men were especially formidable with a bone through their nose, large welts (from initiation into manhood) decorating their torso, and spears in their hand or propped (ready for use) next to them. Each man made his own weapons to fit their own particular height and hand size. When it came to the boomerang, the taller the person the larger or longer the boomerang. Each man's arsenal consisted of at least one spear, spear thrower, shield, a special stick called a wardi, and several boomerangs. The only other things they ever made were ceremonial sticks and various items the witch doctor used in his practice. Their stories and legends were preserved to a great extent through their circle drawings on each man's own sacred sticks.

They neither had nor made such things as chairs, tables, or beds, nor did they grow any crops.

For quite a while at Cundeelee we had only a couple of chairs for the adults, and a tea chest to serve as a table. I soon thought it normal to sit on the soft red dirt; it was only after we moved into a house did I sit using a chair, but only inside the house. Any time I was outside, which was most of my waking hours, to sit meant on the ground whether it was summer or winter. I had also learned to take a nap on the ground in the shade, but only after checking the surrounding area for tracks of snakes or other such critters.

They were knowledgeable and quick to build a fire when necessary in order to cook an animal, or to keep warm, but not just for the "fun" of sitting in front of one. In the Outback it was not necessary to have a fire every day since a lot of the food was eaten raw, and the weather very similar to that of Phoenix, Arizona. Two of the reasons not to make a fire for several days were - not wishing to advertise their presence in the area until they were long gone, and animals smelling the smoke and moving further afield making hunting more difficult. All it took was a dry round smallish branch, a piece of almost flat wood, a few pieces of well dried items, such as animal droppings, two fast hands, some gentle blowing and fire was born. After seeing matches used a couple of times, the Aborigines started asking Dad for the "magic" wood that made fire starting so easy and so very fast.

There were other tribes, but the two largest ones to roam in out and around Cundeelee were the Wangatha and Pitjantjatjara - named after their particular dialects.

Aborigines were for the most part a very stoic people, laughing some, crying rarely to never.

They lived one day at a time with no goals, other than finding food for the day, and no set agenda. Normally they were a quiet people who came and went with swift gracefulness and in almost total silence. However, when death occurred they had an unforgettable blood curdling, desolate and bleak sounding wail. It raised the hair on the back of my neck and arms at its' "forever lost" sound.

In their culture questions were rarely asked, instead they tended to wait, and watch for things to unfold, at which time they would try to figure out how they thought the person wanted them to respond. When questioned they rarely gave an answer that showed how they really felt; instead they tried to give the response they thought would please the person. If the person asking the question happened to be white and arrogant, if the person was cheeky, or condescending towards them, the information or directions given would most likely be incorrect in order to try and teach them a lesson in humility.

Although they were naked when they lived in the bush, the males did have certain coverings, which they wore once they entered into puberty and adulthood. While they lived at or near the station, they wore pants, shirts, and dresses that had been donated to the mission for them. However, when it was time to do some serious hunting, off came the clothes. During a hunt, clothes were considered only a nuisance for they not only hampered quick easy noiseless movements, but they also were not as good a camouflage as was their natural skin. Most of the time they liked wearing clothes as protection or insulation from the harsh elements. Clothes also helped to hide their sores from the pesky and ever present flies. One time while I was still living at Cundeelee, the mission was sent a large box full of gently used large and extra large cotton dresses. Mum thought this would be an ideal opportunity to teach the Aboriginal ladies a little about hygiene. For the first time in their lives each lady would be given two nice clean dresses.

According to Mum's thinking it was time for them to learn to change their one and only dirty dress for a clean one. Now to their way of thinking, if one dress helped to keep the sun and wind from touching their skin, then three would do a lot better job. They also reasoned that no one could steal their new dresses from them while they were out hunting, if they wore all of them all of the time. There was also the fact that if a death occurred while they were out hunting, and "camp" or home had been moved while they were gone, they had no worries for they had everything they owned with them at all times. I knew one old lady in particular who was a typical example of their thinking, for after several years she owned five dresses. She wore them all - night and day, nor could she be convinced to take even one off to wash it. All of her life, water had been in short supply and so precious, that she couldn't even begin to comprehend the idea of wasting water just to wash a piece of material. Water meant survival; a dress was a non-essential.

When living way out in the bush, before they had ever seen a person of another race, the Aborigines made themselves headbands by rubbing rabbit hair between their hands until it became a thin rope. Usually a headband was between five and seven twists of this rope around the head. Its main purpose was to catch sweat in order to cool their bodies as they walked, but it was also a type of decoration. They loved bright colors, and once when mum received a batch of red yarn they asked to have it. Red headbands showed up everywhere.

They did not have a written language, so not being able to read they told stories about everything touching their lives, drawing on the ground as they talked. After a foraging trip it was customary for a group to gather and sit or lay together on the ground under the shade of a tree. Using a stick or a finger people would take turns describing and sketching in the dirt the route taken and where food had been found. Many things were shared – from tracking an animal to funny happenings taking place during the day.

While I was there a linguist from Wycliffe Bible Translators came to start translating their dialect. One day after he had been there a while, he asked us to get everyone together for he had something to show us. What he wanted to show us was a large piece of white paper he had sectioned off into nine squares. Each square had a drawing with a Wangatha word under it. I believe seven of the words were – ear, eye, foot, leaf, nose, tooth, and snake. Whenever I recall the memory of seeing those drawings, I always think of the words in "my" dialect and not the English equivalent. I thought, talked, and lived with their language as my own; however, since it was not a written language, I never learned to read or write it. It was estimated their language at this time in their history consisted of approximately ten thousand words. The Wangatha dialect only had words to count up to three, after which we used the word "many." It made for problems in accurate counting for anyone wishing to know any exact amounts of such things as miles, days or items, but it was irrelevant to us.

These "stone age" people had their own type of sign language, which was used much of the time in place of any verbal communication. Since so many conversations took place in silence, and with small quick gestures such as pointing with the chin or lower lip, or the turn of a hand, I learned to pay attention to subtle movement. When they were out hunting, especially for the larger meat, it was very serious business, and could mean eating or going hungry for a lot of people; therefore hunting was quiet business until after the kill. Hand signals were flashed when fresh tracks were found, signaling what was being followed. If hunting had netted nothing, then on returning to camp a hand signal warned to leave them alone for a while.

These Aborigines had many legends including one of a great flood over the whole earth. They had words for God who lives in the sky, and is ALWAYS GOOD, and for the Devil who works on earth, and is ALWAYS BAD; but they had no words or knowledge of JESUS CHRIST, the Son of the LIVING GOD.

People often asked my Dad (many times in my hearing) why he felt he had to go so far away to tell people about Jesus? Why couldn't he stay in America, where it was safe, near family and not such a hard life?

In my sister's book one chapter tells in detail about an Aboriginal man named Jerry, who lived way back in the interior of Western Australia. He really wanted to know the Good God, but knew no one to tell him. One night Jerry had a dream in which he saw things he'd never seen in his life before. He saw a white man, holding a black book, and he was told the man he saw in this dream would tell him about the GOOD GOD that was written about in the thing he held in his hand. The next morning he told his people about his dream and sent out seven men to go in different directions in search of this man. Whoever found this white man was to return to a certain place at a certain time of year. Year after year Jerry returned – he was now old and this would be the last time he would make this journey.

What do you say to someone who asks if your father, and grandfather, knew about this Holy book, and why no one ever came in time to tell his father and grandfather about the Good God and His son Jesus. This was the question Jerry asked my Dad.

Fear of some sort ate at them every day of their lives. First there was the normal abiding fear of not finding enough food or water in order to survive each day. There was always a fear of the evil spirits in regards to their physical well being or continued well being since the witch doctor might "point a bone" and say "you are dead." We were there when such a thing happened, and in days the cursed individual died – literally frightened to death. There was a dread type of fear that someone's dead spirit would return to "get you" through say, the dead person's dog. There was always the fear of the survival of the fittest especially when food was scarce or one was sick. Their worst fear of all is common to every person who has ever lived on earth, but especially to ones without knowledge and hope of an eternity with God. It was and is the fear of death, dying and the question of what then?

My folks did not realize it, but I so identified with these people that I not only came to understand their fears, but I also started to believe, feel and experience some of those same fears and superstitions myself.

Family & Feet

The Aborigines absorbed us four children into their tribe, assigning us relatives, including grandparents. Being made a part of the tribe brought with it the requirement to obey their laws.

Many immigrants who had come to find work in Australia had often ended up working on the railroad line far away from civilization. In some cases, when an Aboriginal female crossed their path the result was a child born with a lighter colored skin. I mention this simply because they were accepted as one of the tribe with their light skin, so as I grew up I had no reason to believe that my light skin was any different. Since this is where my memories of life began, I considered them to be my people, and their style of life I thought of as being the norm. My upbringing was very primitive in the extreme with no electrical gadgets of any kind, no bicycles or pets or music.

In our home we only had, as I remember, one small mirror, which Dad used when shaving each morning. Mum braided or combed my hair in the morning and I was set for the day. I had no need of a mirror, so I didn't "see" myself regularly each day while growing up. I noticed other's appearance, but never thought to see what I looked like. In my culture to look in the mirror was a non-essential, since what I looked like could not be changed. It was to be accepted without question, and ignored, in favor of learning such important essentials as hunting for food and being able to survive alone if the need arose. In this culture learning by copying was much more important than figuring out "the why" of anything that had already taken place and was not changeable, such as what one looked like.

They had a system sort of like A B C D, in which everyone was assigned a place, to make sure that in the future there would be no incorrect intermarrying. Girls at birth were "given or promised" to a living male. At the birth or time the promise was made the male could be young or very old. Only if he died before she was of marrying age, which was about thirteen, could she marry someone else – still only out of the right group of course. One couple didn't obey these rules, and "ran off" together, knowing they would be hunted down. Tracking them down took over two years and covered half of Australia. They were found and speared for disobeying the tribal laws.

I didn't know until much later that as children we had someone assigned to watch over each of us like a guardian angel. His main duty was to keep us from seeing anything considered to be sacred, and to protect us if necessary from any harm. The protection was not in relation to anything except the tribe as individuals and their laws, and did not cover "white" people at all.

This "guardian angel" could be speared because of something we did, or if we were harmed in any way by one of the tribe, while we were considered to be under their care.

Everyone was known as to who they were and where they had come from and gone to by their distinct footprints being "read" in the dirt. The white people who wore shoes were also known even when they came home with new shoes. While the pattern of their shoe soles was noted, it was the way in which they walked that gave away the important information. Shoes could be changed, but in the dust the way a person walked on their toes, heels, hurried and so on would be picked up on immediately. The person's identity was known without a visual sighting ever taking place.

The only argument I ever remember having with my Aboriginal friends was over footprints. Mine to be precise. I remember the incident well since we had a government agent there that day, and he said he didn't believe it was a "white child speaking the Abo's language." I had been staying relatively close trying to listen in and figure out what the agent was talking about to Dad.

At the same time I was busily engaged playing the tracking game with my little friends. I was normally a quiet easy going child; however, I had just had my footprint referred to as "a foot of the bad devil" so was hotly protesting in Wangatha. Almost all of the Aborigines had wide flat feet, but I had a very high arch, toes that barely touched the ground, and a small foot, which appeared to them as if a big part of my foot was missing; therefore, my footprint was considered to be "spooky." Now anything the least little bit spooky, from a whirlwind to something different and out of the ordinary, was attached in their mind to be the work of the evil devil and would be referred to accordingly. I had learned I could disagree with someone; however, I was not to question "the why of something." I now knew my footprint was different from theirs, and although I had no idea why, I knew to just accept it since it could not be changed. For a bit it looked as if "foot of the bad devil" would become my name. However, after some thought, the "powers that be" decided to name me "wild pear" instead, for they did not want to "wish evil" on me by giving me a bad name for something I had no control over.

Each time Dad received a message over the short-wave radio to bring in (to Kalgoorlie) the best Aboriginal trackers, it meant someone was lost or missing. Over the years many Aboriginal men from Cundeelee gained fame because of their amazing ability to track people - regardless of terrain. They were skilled at determining whether the person was sick or well, in a hurry or not, about how long in hours or days since the tracks had been made, and the direction taken. Many times there were no clear prints for miles, yet they were able to spot where even a few stones had been moved and follow the correct trail. One day, due to "hopping the rails" and getting off at Zanthus, an Aboriginal fellow was riding only the return trip to Cundeelee, with Dad. Watching the side of the road as they traveled, he spotted a footprint (in the dirt beside the road), which he hadn't seen in about four years, and said to Dad "Frank is here." When they finally pulled into camp, Dad skeptically glanced around taking in the various people sitting by their fires, and sure enough there sat Frank.

One time when a couple of us children were out by ourselves for an exploring, hunting for food sort of walk, we traveled into an area new to us. Playing and hunting for food had our complete attention until it suddenly dawned on us that the strange mounds we were now in the middle of were man made. In icy fear and mounting dread we froze in our tracks as with horrified certainty we realized we were indeed in a graveyard. We immediately and with no hesitation or looking around took out running as fast as we could for home.

The location of a graveyard was kept secret. Any stranger, female or child entered or crossed it at their own peril for they could be killed for what they may have seen. I kept my mouth shut as to where I had been, never telling anyone for I knew I had unintentionally broken their law, and seen something sacred to them. I tried hiding, but quickly realized it was a useless endeavor, and tried instead just to keep a very low profile. It was in vain for the next day I was approached by one of the Aboriginal men, and told they had seen my footprints in the cemetery.

Fear once again coursed through me for in my fear of being found out and punished, I had unbelievably forgotten about my footprints being "at the scene." He went on to say the elders observed from my footprints that I had just been playing, and had left immediately. Since I had not stopped to erase my tracks, investigate any mound or move further into the area, my life would be spared. I was lucky for I was getting a second chance; however, if I went near or into this cemetery again, I would be killed. Children of the Outback had a lot of freedom in some ways; however, a lot of verbal warnings were not given. Death was not a threat, it was a promise, and would be swiftly accomplished whether by fear, or a spear. I was learning to know, understand, and live by their laws.

Becoming a child of the Outback did not just happen because a child may have been born and lived in the Outback or bush. It was a way of life, and a mental attitude. Children must learn to survive on their own if necessary, by learning many things. One of the first lessons I was to learn was to be aware of my surroundings. Being alert to what or even who was close to me, whether I was at play or looking for food was an important lesson. Health wise I learned such things as breaking a new switch off of a tree to swat at the flies, and not to use one I had picked up from the ground. As a child of the Outback I learned to recognize which tree roots could be chewed when I wanted a drink and water was not available. I was taught one should never take all the food found from one place, unless it was old or a long trip was ahead. I was learning to read tracks made by humans and animals, and such non-tangible things as not to be greedy, the importance of immediate obedience, of watchfulness and when told to wait to do it with unquestioning patience.

The most important things a child of the Outback learned at a young age was to always use their ears, eyes, and nose, before ever using their mouth. Learning these lessons well was considered a start in becoming a Child of the Outback.

Butter & Bardi

Life for me was always very interesting with so many things to learn, and new food to try, but I had to help find it if I expected to share any of it when it came time to eat. Everything was quite simple. We were always on the lookout for food no matter what else we might be doing. If one knew what they were looking for and where it lived, food could be found almost anywhere, from in the trees, to on, or even in the ground. Men and teenage boys hunted the larger animals such as the wild turkey, emu and kangaroo, using their boomerangs and spears. It was the women and children's job to find, gather and prepare everything else. When hunting, our meat list comprised of such things as birds, lizards, rabbits and snakes. Highest on the list of non-meat food was the bardi grub, which lives and grows in roots of certain shrubs or bushes. They are very high in protein, and can be eaten alive, or after being placed in warm ashes and cooked. The bardi grub, or margoo, as we called it, tasted better as far as I was concerned the larger it grew, and after it had been cooked. The largest one I ever found was about five inches long and a half an inch across. It had a yellowish hard top to its head, many almost imperceptible legs, and a very silky smooth cream colored body.

Large animals were cooked in a pit, whereas everything else was cooked using the hot ashes or the fire itself. No pots, pans or utensils were used, so no water was wasted on washing up. At Cundeelee, large empty tin cans such as the ones "Sunshine Powdered Milk" came in were recycled into useful "billy cans" by adding a wire handle. These tins would be carried on the women's heads whether empty, full of food, or the more precious commodity of the Outback, which was water. Added to our hunting list was anything edible, from roots to sugar found on certain tree leaves, and in between these ranged ants and emu eggs to berries. Due to our lack of water the "berries" were not big, ripe and juicy, but often were only a thin layer of peel covering a pit. After eating the peel, the pit was left to dry in the sun, and it was in this way we gathered enough "clean" pits for a game. Our "board" for any game was the soft red dirt. The games ranged from marbles to one similar to tic-tac-toe, but different in that we drew a square and then a line from corner to corner, and a line each from the top and side to the other side. All lines intersected in the middle, and our aim was to get three of our pits in a row sitting at the end of the lines, or lined up using the center.

Since there were no stores or even for a while no refrigerator for us to go to for food when we got hungry, we learned to find our own snacks in amongst the vegetation around us. In this way I grew up on mostly nutritious snacks, not knowing anything about such things as pop and candy.

I quickly learned to take only enough to appease my stomach, since someone else might need the food left worse than I did, or I might want a snack tomorrow and would know where to find it quickly. Since there was no place to keep extra food, it was a daily adventure as to what I would find as well as its location.

I can remember often hearing my sister telling Mum at meal times that Marilyn had not come in time to set the table, plus now Marilyn was saying she was too full to eat. I did tend to think of anything in the house as belonging to Mum and Darlene and that I fit best outside with my friends and relatives. I dimly realized I was different since I had to go home to a bed every night, but I never stopped to wonder about it. My culture said to accept and move on and not to question, and so as a child I enjoyed being free to roam day after day.

The Aboriginal women carried everything, as much as they possibly could, on their heads, in order to leave their hands free to gather, dig, and swat at the ever present horde of flies. I have a photo taken of me by a new missionary who was amused at how well I had learned the Aborigine's ways. He had been working with Dad in a muddy ditch, and the job being completed had handed me (for I was standing nearby) his overalls, hat, and large rubber boots. I proceeded to put on the hat and boots as I had been taught, trying to keep my hands as free as possible. I remember him looking rather stunned, and amidst much laughter asking Dad what on earth I was doing. I was really rather miffed at him for laughing at me since I was packing his things for him, at a slow shuffle I'll admit, due to wearing his very large rubber boots.

Emu meat while available was usually very tough and so our favorite meat became the tasty kangaroo. At first we ate wild turkey quite a bit, but because Dad was so good at hunting them the government decided to make him a game warden. He became responsible for rationing rather than hunting them. When hunting was really poor, Dad would load the truck with men, their spears and boomerangs, while he took his rifle, and off they'd go. After telling someone at Cundeelee the direction they were taking, they'd be off for the day or until they bagged enough meat to feed the entire camp. Any kangaroo seen but too far away to spear, and big enough to make a good meal became Dad's job with his rifle. At the end of the day all were very thankful for the truck for it made the distance to haul the meat seem so much shorter. Using the truck was definitely easier and healthier than carrying all of the meat back to camp over their shoulders with the flies having a taste first.

Once in a great while in the winter months, then later a little more often after we had a kerosene refrigerator, (which didn't always work) Mum would order butter as a special treat. Actually we had more rancid butter, than fresh on our table in my years there, but whenever we did have butter we really enjoyed eating it on our bread or damper. One day Dale and I hatched and carried out what we thought would be an interesting experiment to try on the new missionaries.

There was a morning "tea" at about ten each morning, another "tea" at about three in the afternoon and sometimes one right before bed. This particular "tea" took place in the afternoon.

If there were no tinned biscuits (cookies) for "tea" then a piece of buttered bread, cut into three or four pieces each an inch or so wide was acceptable. Mum must have suspected something was going on for she had slight frown lines on her forehead, but she didn't interfere since for once we had shown up for tea, and appeared to be helping. We were very careful to take the plate of bread, which we had specially prepared, only to the new missionaries. We hovered close enough to them to offer them more, but far enough away to be able to watch their faces intently without being obvious about it. As conversation lagged one mumbled, "I didn't know there was butter in camp," and Mum being hard of hearing, didn't catch what was said. We started to make a silent and hasty retreat, but Dad had heard and came to check it out. He took one look, and figured out that we had broken open, removed head and skin from several large bardi grubs and spread the innards, which had a color and texture between rancid and real butter, on their bread. He wanted to laugh, to spank us, to just not say anything, but from the look on his face they knew something was going on and they wanted to KNOW too. As nonchalantly yet delicately as possible Dad tried to explain to them what they had just eaten. Funny what tricks the mind has over the stomach. They up chucked their tucker in the bushes, and lost their sense of humor for about a week, and oh, yes, we were punished and made to promise to never again try such a stunt.

Once Mum received via the mail several packets of vegetable seeds. Dad dug up a small patch of ground, enclosed it to keep the many wild animals out and planted the seeds. We had no extra water to spare, but all of the dish, wash, and bath (only once a MONTH) water went on this promising patch of green. To this very day I can see those huge, beautiful cabbages, and remember how long and hard we worked to keep both animals and people from getting in and enjoying the produce before Mum pronounced it was ready for consumption. I also remember all the water I carefully recycled and carried so faithfully to the small green patch. The day finally arrived when Mum said one cabbage was ready to be cut, cooked and eaten. She went out with her little knife, with us at her heels, and gently cut the cabbage off at the bottom of its stalk. We all hurried rather triumphantly into the kitchen. As we stood around admiring this big green beautiful looking vegetable, Mum took out a larger knife and started to cut it up into sections.

She was fast, and had cut it in half, and had just started to cut the next section, when we began to holler. The flies, it turned out, loved our soapy water, and had made our beautiful vegetables into their nursery. The interiors of all of the cabbages were riddled with small wriggling larva. This ended our gardening experiment and Mum's dream of fresh vegetables using recycled water.

We had two types of flies to contend with all of the time. There was the tiny pesky fly, which hovered around one's body, but preferred openings such as the eyes, ears, nose, and mouth or better yet - an open sore to enjoy. The other type of fly was referred to as the blowfly. The blowfly was the menace of mealtime for it could drop it's young accurately and swiftly – using only the time it took to fly across the food. My job was often that of chief swatter in order to keep the flies from ruining the food between the time it took to set it on the table or until a lid covered it. Whether eating or just passing a bowl of food around the table, one hand had to be kept waving constantly in a back and forth motion, in an attempt to keep the flies at bay.

Braids & Birds

When we first arrived at Cundeelee we had only one 2000 - gallon water tank, which stored the only water there was to meet the needs of fifty to two hundred and fifty people for an indefinite period of time. There would never be any water bearing wells at Cundeelee, although there were numerous holes dug and or bored by people certain they would find water. Our one tank contained all of the water on our station with which to meet everyone's needs whether it was drinking, cooking, cleaning, or bathing.

We were very dependent upon nature giving us rain and generous people to pay for the train to supply us with water. Sometimes it seemed as though we were caught, as the saying goes, between a rock and a hard dry place.

Mum, Darlene and I wore our hair long and most of the time we kept it braided. Dad preferred us to have long hair ignoring the fact it took extra water to get our hair clean and soap free. Mum had beautiful thick, long hair, which was very heavy. She kept getting terrific headaches, which the doctor said was probably due in part to the weight of her hair, as well as the intense desert heat. His remedy was for her to cut her hair short. Soon between our water shortage, and Mum's headaches, out came the scissors and off came our long hair. Now even our hair was short, not that I minded skipping all that brushing and pulling when braided, due in a part to our lack of water. Our rainfall was usually between three and four inches a year. The fifty-two miles round trip to the train and back, packing a large unsecured tank in the back of an old truck was a challenge in itself. Whether the truck would get bogged down enroute, have a flat, or even if it still had enough guts for another trip, were all seriously considered each time before embarking on a new adventure. The necessity of water always prevailed, and with much prayer the journey was undertaken.

Leaving Cundeelee headed towards Zanthus began with going down a small rocky hill. Next were reoccurring sections of soft red dirt, sand, and harder packed soil until coming to a salt (river) wash about a hundred feet across. When the "wash" was dry, which it was most of the time, it appeared to be a hard packed expanse of shimmering white salt. Its beauty hid the fact that there was just a very thin layer of crust, and some very nasty black gumbo lay just under the crystal white surface. This spot was five miles from my home. The road wandered for the next twenty-one miles through sand hills, over rocky patches, and stretches of soft red sandy dirt with several natural flash flood areas or washes along the route. During the dry time of year the red dust and sand on the road seemed to get deeper and slicker, and with the next rain it became thick mud. The only vehicle available to haul water from the train was an old army ambulance truck with hard sides and a dip in the center of its floor. The truck's fixed sides and roof made loading the tank onto the truck difficult. Even worse was filling the tank with water in such a severely limited amount of overhead space. Before each trip, besides worrying over the truck and wondering if the road was passable, Dad had other concerns as well. Thoughts raced through his mind whether the "Tea & Sugar," as the train was called, had received our water order, and with all of the stops the train made before reaching Zanthus would there still be enough water left to fill our tank.

I seldom thought about our water shortage, and then only when it affected me personally. For instance when it was very hot and the only thing we had was one wet washcloth to pass around to cool off four children. I also thought about water when waiting for it to boil for fifteen minutes and then cool a bit before I could have a drink.

One year we received a lot more than our normal four inches of rain, which resulted in hordes of Kilykilykarri other wise known as budgerigars, coming further inland than usual. At first we were very thankful for the extra water, and truly enjoyed the blanket of beautiful flowers covering our normally desert like landscape. The mood changed somewhat as the water started drying up. At first it was brush fires that were a major concern and soon it was everyone's health.

Hundreds of frantic birds were competing with us for our water.

A big new water tank had just been completed, but the only "top" or covering for it was light netting. Many birds got through the netting and while trying to get a drink got too wet and drowned. They were not only using up the water, but they were also polluting the remaining water in the tank. There was no way to stop so many birds. The missionary adults, in an effort to keep our water relatively clean, took turns climbing a ladder, leaning into the tank and scooping out as many birds as possible. Scooping and handing the birds down to waiting children went on for hours. I remember my efforts to revive the small birds. I talked to the birds as I gently squeeze as much water out of them as possible thus reviving many, much to the frustration of the adults. First off, after they had been revived, and when they were "good again" they just headed back to the water tank. On the other hand the dead ones, were quickly taken away to become someone's meal. None of the adults were pleased with us children in spite of understanding our feelings. I had twelve or so little birds I worked on at any one time and no one had better touch one unless I saw it really was a goner.

Along with my compassionate nature, this was as close to having a new toy to play with or having anything new and exciting happen in my life.

Mum often said I had one characteristic in abundance and that was tenacity. It was especially true if someone told me I couldn't do something due to my lack of size, strength, or being a girl.

I was also very tenacious about not offending anyone, even unintentionally. Unfortunately this trait did not hold true in regards to my schoolwork, which was in English, and seemed to have no relevance to my way of life. With each passing day I became more of a Child of the Outback in my mannerisms, thought processes and speech.

Words & Wangatha

Learning a new language was almost impossible for Mum with her hearing problems, yet she needed to learn in order to be able to work effectively with the women and children. Mum was trying to help with their medical needs, overcome cultural shock, care for three children and a new baby, in a place with no running water, or electricity and no one to turn to for help or advice. It was Stella, a young Aboriginal woman, who started teaching Mum the language. Stella would pronounce words slowly, loudly and very distinctly without turning or dropping her head, as was the custom. It was not polite to look a person in the eye, so Stella would face Mum while seeming to tend Stephen as he lay cradled in her arms. Stella loved to look after Stephen, so Mum took each opportunity to teach her how to care for a baby, starting with keeping the flies away from their face. Months passed and Stella became pregnant, but with each month her regular daily visit diminished until she did not even come once a week, for it was proving to be a difficult pregnancy. The time for Stella to give birth had arrived and it was night when the radio was inoperative, and the Flying Doctor unreachable. The Aborigines, knowing Stella was Mum's friend and that she was in bad shape, did the surprisingly unexpected by bringing her to our home. It was a long night with no nurse or doctor available for advice or assistance and many complications due to the size of the baby and being a breach birth. Mum stayed with her all night praying and racking her brain as she worked to save the life of her friend and baby.

There was no sleeping that night for "little miss big ears." I heard all of the hushed talk, the moans, and the announcement of the birth. There was a sudden deathly stillness, then sobs as I heard, "Dead, the baby is dead." Mom renewed her desperate attempt to at least save Stella; however, at daybreak Stella died, and the chanting and heart rending wailing began. Mum wept, absolutely exhausted and distraught over losing her good friend. It was hard to live in the Outback without having any ability, knowledge, medicine or a doctor to help in time of great need.

On Sunday morning we would walk down to camp, which was located about a mile away, to have a church service in the open air. Eventually we did have some meetings in one of the Quonset huts when the weather was bad, but while I was there we never had a church building as such. I grew up not knowing about church buildings, pews for certain families, socials, nurseries for small children, youth meetings or choirs. I just knew how to pick a good spot away from certain kangaroo dogs, and under a tree that would shade me the entire time it took for someone to play a few choruses and for my Dad to preach from the Bible. Actually Dad didn't so much preach on Sunday mornings as tell stories from the Bible, and then try to explain how the story in the Bible related personally to how we should live. Dad always had one of the Aboriginal men interpret the sermon for him when he spoke; however, one day Dad decided to try and preach the entire sermon himself in their language. Dad kept missing and skipping words, and his sentence structure was pretty weird, but he was doing fairly well all things considered. He wanted to use the verse in Isaiah 1:18 "Though your sins be as scarlet, they shall be as white as snow." A lot of words had to be changed or left out since they for one thing had never seen snow. He tried to make it as simple as he could by saying, "You can be clean, and white." What he did say was "House can be clean, and spear." There was only one letter different between house and you, or spear and white. It was really a matter of the "ng" sound of each word he had gotten wrong. I stopped playing in the dirt and stared at him as I tried to figure out what he had meant to say. I had been able to figure out all of the other variations in the language without too much trouble, but this took a little longer and then I did the unpardonable and giggled. Dad looked right at me then finished up the lesson quickly in a voice that was not quite as assured as it had been. At lunch time when we were sitting at the table, and after the prayer of "thanks" had been said, Dad said, "Okay, Marilyn, what all did I really say today, and how is it said correctly?" It became Dad's practice on Sunday at lunch to go over the "sermon" of the morning to learn what had really been said. He was also checking to see if his kids were listening and understanding the meaning or the message of the story. It soon became the norm in our home when in doubt over a word or its pronunciation to ask Marilyn, for she usually knew the answer. I soon spoke mostly Wangatha at home in order to help my folks learn the language, and maybe also to avoid speaking English. It was not very long until I rarely spoke in English at all.

There was usually one other missionary family with children living at the station when we were there, and although we did at times play together, my main friends and playmates were the Aboriginal children. As a result, I immersed myself in the Aborigines culture and language, until it was the only language I thought in and spoke fluently. With my acceptance into the tribe, and having been given Aboriginal relatives, I began to think of myself as a Wangkai child in almost every way. I learned to focus my attention on such qualities as attitude and character rather than on skin color, survival rather than appearance and people and their needs rather than myself. I really cared about these people for to me they were my family, my friends, and I considered myself to be one of them.

Tires & Tucker

In the six years that I lived at Cundeelee, other than during the school experiment, I was only off of the mission station itself a couple of times. We had two separate, but each a week in length, holidays during the six years. Having no extra money to spend, the only time we went shopping while on holiday that can I remember, was for food. I grew up having no idea of what it meant to "shop;" whether it was for food, clothes or just for fun. I rarely ever saw any money, and had none of my own, since there was absolutely not one place at Cundeelee where something could be bought. In fact, other than the "Tea and Sugar" train that carried a small amount of goodies for its passengers, there was no where to spend any money for over one hundred and sixty five miles from my home. In six year's time I saw several hapenny, pence, thrippence, sixpence, and shilling coins, and once even a pound note, but I had no knowledge of the use, or value of the money.

Due to many things, including the unreliability of our vehicles, there was only once that I was allowed to stay up and go in with Dad to Zanthus to meet the train to pick up our food, and mail.

The Tea & Sugar train had received it's name through the cargo of food it carried and supplied to Outback areas located along the transline, which always included lots of tea and sugar.

Ordering our food each week was completed by filling out a docket slip and giving it to the man running the store on the train. He in turn would hand it in at Parkeston, which was a stop about three miles away from Kalgoorlie. It was at this location that all orders were filled and labeled for the return trip and delivery the following week. The Tea & Sugar seemed to come through our area of Western Australia during the late night, early morning hours. Once in a great while the train went through early in the evening so it was not an exact science as to when the Tea & Sugar would rumble in and out again. The train usually stopped for about two hours in order to accommodate people at each little stop. When a person did not arrive for their "goods" and everyone else's needs had been met, they would "off-load" their supplies at the depot, and the train would leave. Once in a while Dad would arrive at Zanthus only to find the train had gone through early and departed after off loading our supplies. Dad would then have to try the next morning, via the radio, to get our order filled for the following week. Dad liked to be early to everything, and to him being an hour early was better than being a minute late, but circumstances often got in the way. The hazard list ranged from a flat tire to mechanical problems, washed out or flooded roads, getting bogged (stuck), to hitting a kangaroo. Dad tried to always have at least two men in the truck whenever they made a run in to Zanthus. Along with all of the normal tools in the trucks' toolbox, Dad insisted on carrying some very creative ones as well. He liked to have along chewing gum, friction tape, wire, a small hose, and burlap sacks. He also always packed sand mats and two full canvas water bags. One could be seen hanging from the mirror bracket down the side of the truck, and one dangled in front of the radiator. Even on the hottest day the breeze created while driving cooled the water in the bags to a drinkable, though warm temperature and permeated by a strong taste of canvas.

One night or early morning rather, Dad and the truck did not return home as scheduled from a run into Zanthus. Since the roads were not wet, and the mission was short on petrol the decision was made to wait a while before sending out the jeep or a search party. If they had picked up our supplies then they would have plenty of food to eat and water to drink; however, if there had been an accident, and it had happened on the way to Zanthus then we had a very serious situation. We had no way of contacting the men, and no one else living close enough to help us; therefore, the mission couldn't wait too long to do something.

Often during the "wet" season the jeep with its four-wheel drive was needed to meet the returning truck as it had become stuck in the mud. The truck was often left where it was until it dried up a bit, unless of course it was in a wash area or stuck at Goddards' creek. If it was either of the latter then all the available men hopped in the jeep and went along to help push and pull the truck out. This time however if they had not walked in under their own steam, or brought the truck in within another twenty four hours, then a few of the fast walking Aborigines would take the road to Zanthus in search of them. The missionaries got together and prayed, and then went about the necessary tasks at hand. Some of us kids waited and watched the morning away, taking turns sitting and standing at the top of the hill in the shade of the gum trees, trying to be the first one to hear or see the truck coming.

With no phones, radios, vehicles or even any planes flying over, it was peaceful and so still we could hear things coming while they were a great distance from Cundeelee.

On the way home from Zanthus, due to age as well as the heavy load of supplies on board, the truck's worn-out tires all had blown. The two men had at first felt beaten and depressed with this latest setback, knowing we really needed the food and supplies at Cundeelee. This time the tires had so many holes in them that they were fit only for the rubbish tip. There were no spares available, either with them, or at the mission. Dad had gotten out of the immobilized truck, pulled out his little Bible from his shirt pocket for he always carried it with him, and sat down in the shade of a tree. He read a bit from his "black" book, and prayed to Jesus for guidance and help. While sitting there praying an idea popped into his mind to put sand and gunny sacks in the tires, wire the holes closed, keep the speed as slow as possible, and "give it a go."

Along about two or three in the afternoon, for the sun was no longer in the middle of the sky, we first heard, and then spotted our old truck moving ever so slowly towards us. It seemed peculiar for there appeared to be a blue haze surrounding the truck. We waited and watched, discussing what we thought we saw, until its nearness and our curiosity took over, at which time we all ran down the hill to meet, greet and check out the truck for ourselves. The tires on the truck were all smoking, or were they? Looking closer as we ran and danced between the spinifex and the slow moving truck, we saw the big holes with sacks poking out of the truck's tires. Dad's creative toolbox had come in handy once again and this time it was a combination of prayer, sacks, and wire that had met the need.

That night at the supper table Dad was pretty discouraged over this latest setback, knowing there was no money – especially for tires. I wasn't paying much attention, but Dale remembers Mum telling Dad not to worry, for she had been assured while praying that a check to cover the cost of a complete set of new tires was even now on its way. She referred to the verse in Isaiah 65:24, which says, "Before they call I will answer; and while they are still speaking I will hear." Dale told me that at the time he said to himself, "I don't think God is interested in tires - lets see just how long it takes for God to answer."

In the mail the following week was a letter that read something like, "while praying I felt suddenly constrained to write you a check specifying it is to be used for truck tires. Would you be kind enough to write and tell me what is going on, and if tires are needed."

Finally the night came, the only one ever for me as a matter of fact, when I was allowed to go with Dad to meet the train at Zanthus. Dad actually took a number of us children with him that evening, making sure we started early enough to ensure our seeing the train arrive in all of its puffing, cinders, and noise.

When we arrived at Zanthus we played for a bit under the huge old pepper trees next to the railway lines, and as previously instructed, ran to stand by our truck when we heard the train coming. We were to stay by the truck until the train had pulled in and stopped. It was during this time Dad surprised us by giving each of us one shilling (a shilling equaled twelve cents) and a six pence or eighteen cents to spend! One car of the train had a small built in store stocked with goodies such as confectionery, candy, pop, cigarettes, sometimes some fruit, and we were going to get to explore its bounties. We had only the time it took to off load the supplies from the train to the truck in which to make our choice from the store and get back to the truck. There were so many things to choose from. I hadn't seen anything like this before, didn't have a clue as to what anything would taste like, didn't want to waste my only money and couldn't make up my mind. My mind felt stunned with choices. The fellow in charge kept a sharp eye on us, just in case we might "lift" anything. After a child had spent their money they were promptly shooed out the door, until I was the only one left staring at all these foreign items. I knew I had to hurry but felt paralyzed to make a quick decision, for there were so many things from which to choose. What lay under the "skin" of each colorful wrapping? Were they all edible treats? I was only going to have this one chance to choose something. I wanted to enjoy what I bought and not waste my precious money. In the end it was due to the attendant's help, and not a word spoken by me, that I traded almost all of my money for a candy bar, and an orange crush soda pop which came in a glass bottle. Dad arrived as I hurried down the steps clutching my treats, and the attendant nodded at Dad and said we'd been "right good," which meant that we would be welcome to come again.

By the time we had traveled the twenty-six miles home it was very late or rather early in the morning, and everyone had finished their "tucker" except Marilyn. I rode all the way home tightly clutching my treats for I wanted to savor them for as long as possible. Normally I would share anything I had with anyone, but not this time. They had eaten theirs, and they were not getting mine, even if the chocolate was melting, and the pop was loosing its fizz. Over the next several days I would stick my tongue into the bottle and tip it just enough for the liquid to touch my tongue. This small taste I considered to be my treat for the next several hours. Despite threats and pleas I eked out, protected, and enjoyed to the full my special treats. I was able to make them last a week, after which time I returned to hunting happily "my" type of bush treats each day.

Doctor & Doll

Our only link to the outside world for medical advice, to send and receive messages, and for listening to the School of the Air was our short-wave radio. Each day our radio reception was nonexistent from about four in the afternoon, all through the night, and finally came good again at about nine the next morning. All radio conversations, whether private or not could be heard in homes all across the outback of Australia. In this way although we were so very far apart in distance, we heard about the joys and the trials of people in Outback settlements across Western Australia.

Through the radio we knew when others needed water, the flying doctor, trackers, or when to look out for people driving our way. To watch out for them could mean anything from keeping an eye open for smoke from their fire, dust from their vehicle, or even when out hunting to watch for their tire tracks. It did not always mean we had to see them face to face to report that they had "gone through" our area. If they hadn't checked in at their next scheduled stop in a day or so, then to watch out for, changed completely. If they were believed to be in our area, we were asked to send out a search party immediately to find out if they were in trouble. They could be stranded due to an accident with a roo, bogged down in mud or sand, out of petrol or water, to having taken the wrong direction, and their survival could now depend upon someone finding them, and quickly. There were always a few who had just decided to camp longer in one spot and lacked consideration for others for they knew people would start a search.

Every outback station or homestead was equipped with a special medicine chest full of numbered medicines. After describing the patient's obvious symptoms to the Flying Doctor via the short-wave radio, he would in turn prescribe what number of medicine in the chest to take, how often, how many and what reactions might occur. Only something real major would result in a trip to hospital, and so we learned to care for ourselves. Such things as a fight resulting in a spear through a leg, a split open head, to the scratch on my leg, which became two inches long and an inch deep after turning septic - all these "emergencies" were treated via the radio, and numbered medicines.

It seemed as if I was always having earaches and tonsillitis, but usually the medicine prescribed by the doctor via the radio, soon put me right again. Early one afternoon Mum found me rolling my head back and forth on our bumpy steamer trunk, and at once saw that I was not playing, but moaning with pain. My throat hurt and once again I had shooting pains in my head spiking from both ears. It felt as if each stab increased the pain and built even more pressure in my aching head.

At almost the same time another little girl my age was acting very strangely. Some thought it could be her appendix; however, since no one had any medical training, no one was really sure what was wrong with her. Once again in retrospect I see God's protection over us, as it was before 4 PM that our symptoms became apparent and Dad was able to reach the Flying Doctor for advice. At this time Cundeelee did not have an airstrip.

Since it was basically life or death for my friend, the Doctor said get both of us to the railway line as soon as possible. He also told Dad that he would take care of making sure the train stopped and waited if necessary, until we got to Zanthus. Here was another miracle for this was the day it wasn't the slow Tea & Sugar, but the fast train that would be going past Zanthus, and it would be coming through that very evening. Things were now moving along to get us to hospital, but the hard part still lay in front of us. Cundeelee Mission Station still owned only two vehicles, which were the huge old army ambulance truck, and a jeep. It had to be the truck with its relatively flat floor. The bed of the truck was separated down the middle by a large wide dip of about eight inches deep and two feet wide and ran the length of the bed. Our Mothers kissed us before we were each wrapped up in a blanket and placed on individual army cots and strapped onto the cot. Our cots were then lifted and placed one on each side on the floor or bed of the truck for the first part of our long journey.

The army cots had been designed to slide into the metal grooves down each side of the truck bed and thus held in place during transport. Due to constant use hauling such things as water tanks and sandalwood, the runners were twisted and bent inward and unusable in this crisis situation.

There were no doors on the back of the truck, and our cots with us in them would be in constant danger of sailing off into the road or the bush along the roadside. Dad, known as the best truck driver on the station, was chosen to drive this emergency run. The largest Aboriginal man I ever knew volunteered to sit on a blanket in the middle depression of the truck bed and hang on to our cots for the entire trip. The families gathered for prayer, Dad got into the driver seat, and I watched as my good friend stretched out his arms and then wrapped a large hand around the metal tube on each cot. We were set to rock and roll and roll we did as we started down the first hill. It was a comfort amidst the pain to be strapped down and to know that a friend was doing his best to keep our cots from sliding off the end of the truck. In the best of times our rough road bounced passengers around a fair bit, and now we needed all of the TLC the truck and driver could give us. The trip was almost as taxing on Dad driving as it was on us in the back. He wanted to drive "flat out" or as fast as he could, but knew he had to slow down and try to avoid hitting as much as possible all the potholes, ruts, rocks, and shrubs growing in the road. I was not critical, but my friend was, and every bounce could have been one too many. Our cots slid back and forth, fell into the middle depression, and bounced out again, making it an excruciatingly long pain-racked trip.

Other than the drone of the engine, our moans, and an occasional sharp mutter from the man so faithfully holding onto our cots, it was a pretty silent trip. As soon as our truck headlights were spotted the conductor notified the engineer, and the minute the truck stopped the conductor was there to lend a hand. By this time my little friend had been unconscious for quite a while.

In very short order the straps on our cots were undone, we were carried to the train and placed on bench like seats. Dad did a quick check to see that the little girl was still alive, patted me, and disappeared with the conductor. The train started to roll, and we were now a mere one hundred and thirty miles from the hospital.

Now we were alone, just two small sick girls traveling together on the train towards the hospital.

We had been wrapped up tightly in blankets and laid on seats that faced each other. I wriggled enough to get a peek hole so I could see what was going on, but at the same time stay hidden.

The conductor checked on us from time to time just to make sure we were still breathing, for he knew we were sick and supposed to be "off loaded" when the train arrived at the

Kalgoorlie Station. Hours later when we arrived in Kalgoorlie, we were still wrapped up in blankets from our heads to our toes. When they picked me up to carry me to the waiting ambulance, I remember thinking they were going to drop me. They were being so careful with my feet, while my head was hanging down almost to the ground.

The next thing I remember was arriving at the hospital where they removed the blanket, placed me on a cold metal trolley, and wheeled me into a huge cold room. I was left all alone in the room for what seemed to be an eternity. It probably was a long time since it was a small hospital and they were busy trying to save my friends life for her appendix had ruptured. I had plenty of time to check out my surroundings. I saw all sorts of cruel looking instruments, some of which had jagged edges while others looked to be very sharp. I was so very scared, and wished to get up and run out of there, but once again I had been strapped down tightly. I could hardly move. No one was with me to comfort or to tell me what I was doing there or even what was going to happen to me. I was shaking with fear and also due to the coldness of the room, but I would not allow myself to cry for it was not acceptable behavior. Finally some people came into the room. They were all dressed in what looked like crisp white overalls with masks over their faces so I could see only eyes. To this child of the outback it was definitely in the very spooky realm. After muttering to each other words I didn't understand they put an evil smelling cloth over my nose. I tried desperately to wiggle my head free and away from the awful smell, but a set of hands grasped my head and held it still.

When I woke up I was propped up in bed with my head wrapped in hot cloths, which made my ears feel better; however, I now felt very sick to my stomach, still had a very painful throat and also had a pain in my side. Between bouts of throwing up, and eating Jell-O and ice cream I took stock of my new surroundings. Although I could not see my friend and felt too ill too move, my eyes and ears were very busy taking in the weird sights and sounds around me.

The hospital I was in had a very well organized system in which to get people up and walking as well as be of help to the nurses. The only segregation was whether one was in the women's or men's ward. The first day I was allowed to be lazy, and watch what everyone was doing. Other than a male nurse with a bad limp, who had no tender loving care when he jabbed the needle in your bottom, it was a painful, but uneventful day. The next morning I, along with almost everyone else was handed a flat piece of cotton batting about 12" x 18" x 1" and expected to make it into cotton balls for use in the hospital. Since I had watched my roommates carefully the day before, I now copied them by pulling a piece from the batting, then placed it between my hands and rolled it into a ball. In this way I was able to occupy the morning without saying a word, and when my last piece had turned into a little ball, I was allowed to rest and have lunch.

On the third afternoon it was time for me to "rise and shine" or in other words to get out of bed, to straighten up, and walk. Each time I sagged forward I was encouraged to take another step by a ruler being pushed into my back by a nurse. I couldn't figure out what was wrong with me since I was now hurting in more places than when I had arrived. The fourth morning I received a smaller piece of batting, only to find out it was now my turn to carry a pillowcase from bed to bed, filling it with the finished cotton balls. This job accomplished two purposes; to get me out of bed and on my feet, and the cotton balls picked up without wasting any nurses' time. I liked going around picking up from the women, with their "love," "dearie," and "how are you chooks," but I was scared to go on the men's ward. The "sister" or nurse had to push me gently a couple of times to get me into their ward, which of course set off the bored and hurting men. Some wanted a wee bit of fun, and wouldn't put the cotton balls into the sack, but said I had to pick them up myself, then would try to grab my hand when I reached for the cotton balls. Others, before they would allow me to take the cotton balls, wanted me to say something in any language saying they didn't think I could talk.

Probably everyone in the outback with a short-wave radio knew more about what was going on than I did. All I knew was that a stranger came into the ward with the Matron, who told me I could leave the hospital now, but I'd be staying in town with this lady until my friend was well enough for us to travel home together on the train.

I did not know this lady; or her me, yet being told by the matron who to me was the person in authority here, I went with the lady unquestioningly, albeit a little fearful. This "town lady" told me her children were all boys, so she would be delighted at having a small girl in her house for a few weeks. She bought me a doll whose eyes opened and closed, and would walk with me when I held its hand. We even went shopping for a few clothes, which she said she really enjoyed, as it was more fun than shopping for boys all of the time! I didn't understand at the time why I had to stay with this family, so just kept hoping and trusting that if I was a real good girl and did what I was told, I would soon get to go home. It was another two weeks before I finally got home, and once again it was via the train and truck. On arriving home I ran inside to Mum and the first thing I said was "LOOK," pulled up my dress and showed her my scar. Mum almost fainted. My appendix had been removed instead of my tonsils, which I have to this very day, and they still at times become inflamed.

I had survived living with strangers yet again. I personally had no clear understanding as to why or how long I was to stay with them. I wasn't too sure being good was what had helped me to get home fast, but figured I was now home for good. Little did I realize this was yet another small step in preparing me for much longer, unexplained separations from my family that would take place in a couple of years.

Poem & Punishment

My sister Darlene was very helpful to mum, as well as being very bright, conscientious, and studious when it came to her schooling. My brother Dale and I were very good at playing, and not good at doing our schoolwork, which was by correspondence and with little supervision.

During the next few years, school to me meant pages of papers. Every subject had a page or two of questions with a place for answers under each question. One problem with this type of learning was due to the fact that we didn't know how we had done until two weeks after we had completed the lesson. Every week or two we would send in our finished lessons rolled up in a large sheet of white paper with our name, mailbag number, and station on the outside. The same train taking our completed lesson to the teacher returned via number eight mail bag with our previous and now corrected lesson, plus our new lesson. It was in this way each child on correspondence across Australia sent and received their schoolwork. Darlene would go over and over and over her lessons until she wore holes in the paper with her erasing in an attempt to get each lesson perfect. Dale usually sat down the last day or two and whizzed through his with little care, and though he didn't do too badly, his lessons were usually returned with "needs to spend more time." Being only in the first standard (grade) I was getting help with my lessons from Mum and my sister. Other than at lesson time, I rarely heard any English spoken at all. I never read anything except what was needed to complete my lessons, and so my scholastic difficulties began. Once in a great while we were able to tune the radio in to the School of the Air out of Perth, but all I remember was the teacher using radio call numbers and hearing children's voices answer, but she never used our 9EK call numbers.

It was a couple of years before we got a certified teacher at Cundeelee. He did not understand us or we him, nor did we wish to, since "he" had removed our freedom so to speak. Instead of roaming free we were now stuck inside a building for the better part of a day.

We had not run by time or a clock since arriving at Cundeelee, and only realized the passing of a week when we had "church" in camp each Sunday morning. Dad and Mum had watches, and I think we may have had one clock in the house, but I don't remember seeing any as time had little meaning in my world.

One thing about this teacher forever stamped in my memory is a funny poem he taught us to say and the accompanying hand movements. I don't know who wrote the poem, but here are the words, which are said using a sort of one, two cadence or slight pause at each comma.

> I wish, how I wish, that I had a little house,
> With a mat, for the cat, and a holey for the mouse,
> And a clock, going tock, in the corner of the room,
> And a kettle, and a cupboard, and a big birch broom.
> To the school, in the morning, the children off would run,
> And I'd give them a kiss, and a penny, and a bun,
> But directly, they were gone, from this little house of mine,
> I'd clap my hands, and snatch a cloth, and shine, shine, shine.
> I'd shine all the knives, all the windows, and the floors,
> Every grate, every plate, all the handles on the doors,
> Every fork, every spoon, every lid, every tin,
> Till everything was shining, like a bright new pin.
> At night, by the fire, when the children are in bed,
> I'd sit, and I'd knit, with a cap upon my head,
> And the kettles, and the saucepans, they would shine, shine, shine, In this teeny, weenie, cozy, little house of mine.

Teachers came and went fast in our area of the Outback for we were considered to have two major strikes against us. The first strike was when they found out they would be required to teach Aboriginal children and the second our isolated location. As the novelty of their situation clashed with the daily reality of flies, lack of water and no shops, they, along with their sense of adventure, quickly departed Cundeelee for an easier post.

In those days if a person wanted to become a nurse, or a schoolteacher, and didn't have the funds, they could sign a contract with the Australian government. When the individual had completed the two years of schooling, which had been paid for by the Australian government, they received a certificate of completion of studies. For the next two years they were expected to serve at whatever post they were assigned to in Australia. It was due to this program that many of the Outback towns received medical help and teachers, in spite of their location. While working off their "loans" they were given a stipend in pounds each month, plus room and board. At the end of the two years they were free and clear of any obligation, and could apply wherever they wished in the country.

Once Cundeelee and Zanthus were simultaneously without a teacher, and the government made a decision to try an experiment and have one teacher for all of the students. The teacher agreed to it as long as he could live and teach in Zanthus and not have to go to Cundeelee where the majority of children resided.

Darlene, being older and way ahead of us in school, had to stay at home and keep on doing correspondence by her lonely self. The rest of the Cundeelee children had to travel the twenty-six miles twice a day to attend the school in Zanthus. At first we didn't mind the twice a day long bouncy drives with our feet hanging over the sides of the flat bed truck, for by this time the top and sides of the truck had been removed. We quickly came, however, to not only hate school, but also to dislike and really fear the teacher.

It wasn't just the Aboriginal children he hated, but us "white" missionary kids as well for being their friends, living with them happily, and for being able to speak their language better than English. His demeanor showed he felt we were beneath him, and that it was a waste of his talents and time to try and teach us anything. The rule in our home had always been if we were punished at school we were spanked at home; however; we felt this was now very unjust since we were being caned on the hands and legs for doing nothing wrong. We were living in fear to speak or not to speak, and Dale's presence especially, for some unexplained reason, seemed to make our new teacher angrier each time he looked in Dale's direction.

The teacher had a very nasty little dog that loved to nip at our heels, and since we didn't wear socks or shoes, we had no protection at all from its sharp little teeth. Not only did the teacher do nothing to stop his dog from these daily attacks, but he also seemed to take delight in watching his dog inflict pain on others. One day, while trying to get away from the dogs snapping teeth,

Dale made a threatening gesture towards it with his hand. Despite his not touching the dog in any way, Dale still ended up getting severely caned by the teacher, "for threatening his dog." Inside I raged and felt like screaming, weeping, shouting, and even wished the teacher to be caned, but outwardly must have appeared not to care. The Aboriginal way was not to show any emotion, which we were striving to do, and as a result we made the teacher even angrier. I remember one Aboriginal child being caned until the teacher was too tired to hit him any longer. At recess we started saying, loud enough for the teacher to hear us, that we'd have him speared for sure. It had taken a couple of months for the adults to see what was really going on in the school.

Then he was gone, and we were not traveling long distances to school anymore for which everyone was thankful. It wasn't just the children who were exhausted from daily emotional stress as well as the traveling, but the whole mission had been affected. The men had interrupted their work in order to drive the truck and then had to waste time waiting all day for us. The old truck was expensive to keep running and guzzled more than its share of petrol. The "experiment" had been very costly, both emotionally and monetarily and thankfully was not repeated again.

It was in 1954 and after the daily check in with the Flying Doctor, who had told everyone listening to hang on and hear an announcement to be made by the School of the Air. It was exciting news for the children living in Outback areas, and not too far from the east to west railway line crossing Australia.

The Queen of England was coming to Australia, and would make a trip via the train across the country stopping at pre-determined places along the route. Since there were a lot of Aborigine children at Cundeelee, Zanthus was named as one of the stops the Queen was to make. We listened to this news on the radio with much excitement, for not only would we get to see the Queen, it also meant an exciting trip to the train with the possibility of some sweets to boot.

Over the next few weeks we were told via the radio what songs to learn, that the boys must learn to bow, and the girls to curtsy. If there were enough children, at any place she was scheduled to stop, an added requirement was to learn how to march in a line or formation. We did pretty well with the first lot of instructions, since they played the songs we were to learn over the radio, but marching was another story. We didn't know our left from our right since we never used those words. Our road was one lane, no rows of homes or shops, and we wore no shoes. If we told someone where something was we either pointed with our lower lip, or drew in the dirt and said "here" or "there." At first we tried to learn left and right, but after mixing them up all the time, finally just tried moving the same way the person in front of us did. We were very good at copying things so did much better with this method of keeping in step than when someone yelled left or right for each step we were to take.

Someone made us a yellow banner with the emblem of a kangaroo on it. The Aboriginal child to give the Queen the expected wild flowers had been chosen. In the mail we had each received our booklets as mementos of this soon-to-take-place historic event in our lives. We were to meet the Queen. Excitement was in the airwaves all along the transline (railroad) at the settlements, and amongst the people and children, as the time was now down to less than a week when we would see the Queen.

Then came that fateful morning when Dad did his check-in via 9EK with the Flying Doctor. It was in this way we heard there been an outbreak of poliomyelitis somewhere along the transline.

The authorities learned of it just in time to cancel the Queen's entire train trip, thus saving her from any unnecessary risk of exposure to the disease. The Flying Doctor went on to say everyone was ordered to cancel any group gatherings they had planned until further notice. As an added precaution Dad was told to try and keep the Aborigines from going "walkabout" as much as possible. We had spent hours learning how to bow, curtsy, sing, and sort of keep in step, but we never even came close to seeing the Queen of England.

This was the first time I experienced such a prolonged period of excitement, which ended only in deep disappointment; however, it would be far from the last.

Homes & Heaven

At the start of the mission one of the first buildings needed was a secure place to store the "rations" from the government for the Aborigines; not that it was secure from all the insects.

Since there were so many things to do, our family started life at Cundeelee living in a tent under a brush shelter. It was close to a year before we were able to move into a house. Our new home was in reality a Quonset hut, but it had firm sides that were not bothered by wind or rain; however, it had no flooring nor at first any partitions. This Quonset hut was made out of corrugated iron and shaped in a half circle, which ended about eight inches up from the ground.

Sleepers (railroad ties) were placed all around the outside, and dirt was heaped up against and over them to try and stop as many critters as possible from entering at will. The floor in our new home was comprised of dirt, just soft red dirt, which was native to the area. The dirt stayed heaped over the sleepers only until the insects, wind and rain created new holes. It was never long before a breeze was once again blowing across the floor of our home, creating holes for anything that crawled or wiggled; an open invitation to visit. Our new home was very hot in the summer and very cold in the winter, but it provided better shelter and more room than the tent had. It was a regular-sized Quonset hut, which to us seemed huge and grand. Dad made lines in the dirt marking where he wanted partitions to be placed to create individual rooms. The walls went up, using only wire and a kind of slate-like material, which as I recall was referred to as canonite. These "sheets" of material came, as I recall, in six foot long, three-foot wide, and about a half-inch thick. The slate was sandwiched between looped wire, which was then twisted to keep it in place. With about a three-foot gap for a doorway into each room, and an old blanket thrown over the top wire of each door for a little bit of privacy the interior decorating was done.

There were a total of five rooms, which included the kitchen, and a hallway that ran the length of the building. The bedrooms were assigned as follows, Mom and Dad, Dale and Stephen, Darlene and Marilyn, and soon six young Aboriginal boys had the last one. The kitchen was rather rustic. A wash basin sat by the front door on top of an upside down well worn, empty wooden tea chest. Next in line were dishes and silverware sitting in separate boxes, on top of other boxes. Up against the partition of our folks bedroom was a large wood-burning stove, and an old icebox (not a refrigerator) sat in the corner. In the middle of the kitchen sat a huge flat board braced underneath with more strategically placed, empty, wooden tea chests.

One night we were awakened suddenly by screams, coming from my bedroom. Darlene jumped out of our bed dragging me with her, sobbing that something had bitten her. After pulling back the sheets, and finding nothing, Dad and Mum flipped the mattress over, and there was a huge centipede. Well, it was about seven inches in length. Darlene calmed down a lot when she knew what had bitten her, since it had not been one of our deadly snakes or spiders. For weeks the bite continued to burn and had the appearance of an infected boil. Because she was sleeping on the outside or edge of the bed, she had gotten bitten instead of me, which sums up the way she lived.

She always tried her best to look out for me, her younger sister.

In the morning, before putting our feet on the dirt floor, we'd lean over the bed checking for tracks to make sure the critters passing through during the night had kept on going. Dad, Mom, and Darlene wore shoes, so each morning they had to hit them hard then shake them out carefully to make sure no creepy crawlers had settled inside for a little nap.

Dad wanted to have a house for us with a proper floor, for he daily worried one of us, and especially baby Stephen, would incur a fatal bite. There was always so much other work to be done. It took a few years, and a few scares, but with Dad's persistence, along with people who came to Cundeelee to work, we finally had a real fancy house in which to live. The new house had two stories, more or less, and most important a cement floor. We even had a few luxuries such as a kerosene refrigerator (that ran more off than on it seemed), and if the generator was running, some light other than a candle or a Tilly (lantern). The bathroom was still the outhouse, out back. We still ran outside to the tank for water, which of course we still had to boil fifteen minutes before it was drinkable. This home actually had a couple of proper doors that closed off the bedrooms. Darlene and I again roomed together, but this time we were on the second floor, which was a grand name for the tiny attic. We were both pleased to finally have our very own cot in which to sleep. One side of each cot was pushed right up against a side of the corrugated iron roof. This gave us a narrow isle in which to walk between the cots. The roof had a small pitch, was not insulated on the inside; the highest point was only fifteen or so inches above our heads, and was made up of thin corrugated iron.

Each day had new adventures, and sometimes they started early. Our new culture was teaching us to stay quiet, calm, and in control – well, as much as possible. One morning I woke up suddenly feeling as if something was definitely wrong. Looking over at Darlene I noticed that she was lying very still, staring at something above her, and so I looked up to see what had her complete attention. About twelve inches above her head was a large hairy tarantula sort of looking down at her contemplating his jump. This spider wasn't even stretched out and measured about six inches across with all of its legs bent up tight. Ho, hum, another day had begun.

Every now and again, and only after much preparation, at a Sunday morning camp service, Dad would try and tell a story without using an interpreter. As time passed I noticed that when Dad really studied and practiced ahead of time he was almost good enough in Wangatha to take the fun out of listening for glaring mistakes. I was now hearing what he was saying from the Bible.

Aborigines, who had never seen a white person before, knew and had names for a Good God, and a Bad Devil. Their language and culture contained much of the same reality of right and wrong as was in "Western" or "Christian" cultures. Life revolved around what was good, what was bad, and the bad devil's influence in this world.

Now I hated thunder and lightening storms, and even being told to think of it as God just moving the furniture around in Heaven, did little to help. During the noisy storms we had encountered, I had thought it was bad enough in the tent, and very much better, although louder, in our old Nissen or Quonset hut, but now my head was less than two feet from the tin roof. The noise from the rain alone was enough to deafen a person, but when that same person is afraid, well, the pounding of my heart would vie with the noise on the tin roof.

It was the middle of the night when once again a terrific wingdinger of a storm rolled through. At the first clap and roll of thunder, I shot straight up in bed just positive it was the final trumpet of the Lord signaling the return of Jesus. My heart was pounding with fear even though I quickly realized it was only another very violent storm. I started thinking, and realized that I had never asked Jesus into my heart to forgive my sins. I knew I was not a perfect little girl, and I wanted to be clean and white inside so I would go to heaven when I died. I quickly climbed out of bed, knelt down and prayed to Jesus to forgive me of my sins, and to make me clean. A feeling of peace swept over me, for according to the Holy Scriptures I was now clean in God's eyes, and I was going to heaven were I to die. With a clean conscience I crawled back into bed and immediately fell into the most peaceful sleep – totally unaware of the racket still going just inches from my head.

Now Mum knew I was very afraid of storms and this one was a dilly so she had gotten up to check on her daughter. She found and lit the Tilly, put a log in the stove so she could fix us something hot to drink, and then climbed the stairs to comfort her daughter. To her complete astonishment, I was not only apparently sleeping peacefully in spite of the awful din, but I even had my head outside of the covers. Checking to make sure I was breathing, and that Darlene was okay, Mum went back down the stairs in stunned amazement. Actually it was the one and only time to this day that I've ever been known to go to sleep or even to sleep during a thunder and lightening storm.

My older brother liked to sit in trees as a sort of quiet time by himself, but his favorite place to hide was a big old burned tree. Lightening had struck it and he had hollowed it out. If he could have a special place to hide then so could I.

In the new home there was a part of the attic, which had a very small closed off crawl space into the eaves. Sometimes two of us little girls, for no more would fit in the space, would go in there to just sit on the rafters and chat, or even to hide from someone.

Trousers & Truth

I learned early that life for me was never going to be a "bed of roses" as well as the fact that my circumstances were not the norm, and they often seemed very unfair. There were people that came into my life making decisions of their own that not only affected me adversely at the time, but also almost succeeded in forever destroying me emotionally. I struggled with the fact that nothing bad, that I knew of, happened to them personally. It was only much later in life I realized that now the "ball was in my court" so to speak, and I had to make a choice as to how I was going to let my past affect my future.

At Cundeelee we often had people arrive calling themselves missionaries and saying they were there to help in any way that was needed. There were a few that came wishing only to use their mouth, voice or instrument, and never dirty their hands with work, let alone get close to an Aborigine. For these few it was for the experience and "bragging rights" when they returned to the city, and not out of concern for the Aboriginal people that they were there. I was ten or eleven when one such white man "missionary" arrived to "help out" at Cundeelee.

My little friends and I had noticed from time to time that he seemed to have trouble remembering to do up his zipper, and he wore no underwear. Now we knew the difference between girls and boys, since the small Aboriginal children ran around naked. The adolescent and adult Aboriginal males were very careful never to "show" themselves, even when they were fresh out of the bush where they had been naked all of their lives.

One day, two of us little girls were playing in my bedroom in the attic when we heard a man enter the house and start up the stairs. We could tell by the sound of his boots and his smell as to who was coming up the stairs. Other than my father and brother, no male had been up in the attic since the day we had moved in, so we knew something was not right, especially since he was trying to be so quiet. We immediately scurried to the crawl space; darted in, pushed the panel closed and huddled as far away from the panel as we could get. We took turns peeking out through a crack to see what he was doing. What we saw troubled us greatly. He did not say anything. He didn't move about. He just sat staring at where we were hiding. After much quiet whispering in a mouth to ear exchange, we finally figured out what to say using English words.

We said in unison and very loudly, "He ought to do up his trousers" for he was "showing himself." We felt shamed for him, for only little children would ever be caught doing such a thing. We stayed where we were waiting for him to do up his zipper and leave. We couldn't understand why he hadn't taken our hint and left, but he was in no hurry to do so until a human-made noise occurred near the house. After hearing the sound he stood up, zipped up his pants, and tiptoed oh so quietly down the stairs. We waited until he had been gone a long time, just in case he was still nearby, before we came out of hiding.

We didn't understand why he had come upstairs, or what he had wanted, but we did not trust him because of his body language and sneaky ways. It would be shameful to us as well as to him to mention his bad habit. We thought it was accidental, and since we were not tattletales, in the following days we did our best to ignore, avoid, and even purposely looked the other way each time we saw him.

For a brief time there were goats at Cundeelee kept penned up about a mile down the hill from the ration hut and mission buildings. It was my brother Dale's job to milk the goats each morning. Dale was sick one morning, and how this man knew I never found out, but he showed up at our house. Each time I had seen him I had tried to avoid him, but this time I was in the house and standing right beside Mum. He sounded so willing to help as he told Mum that he would milk the goats. He threw in as a sort of after thought, that Marilyn could show him where the pens were, claiming not to know their location. I begged Mum in a whisper (which she could not hear) not to send me, and sent her a pleading look that she did not see. How could I explain only a gut feeling that he was a bad man, when I did not know that bad men existed!

Mum had people clamoring for her attention, a sick child, and now a reluctant one as well. She thought it a little strange, for while I was often reluctant to do things inside, I had never turned down a chance for a walk in the bush. As Mum picked up and handed me the milk pail she said, "just show him where the pens are and come back."

As a child I was completely at home in the bush, knew where most footpaths around Cundeelee led, and for some reason never lost my sense of direction. It had taken me a while to realize that not all people had this ability and so it was with reluctance that I headed down the slope. On our walk down to the pens where the goats were I made sure to keep well ahead and on the opposite side of the footpath, in other words, well out of his reach.

All went well until we reached the pens and I tried to hand him the milk pail. He grabbed my arm for a second, then released me saying that I would have to wait and take the milk home, because he was expected somewhere else, and wouldn't be going back in that direction. I did not like it at all, for Mum had said come right back, but I had been taught to obey my elders. Since I wasn't speaking or hearing much English I figured maybe he had not said that, for there was no other place to go except back to Cundeelee as everything radiated from there. I stayed outside the large solidly enclosed pen comprised of sleepers on top of sleepers. I wandered around watching the colorful bantam rooster, the chooks otherwise known as chickens, and the goats, with quick side-glances at him every now and then. When he finally called me to come and get the milk pail, he appeared to be distracted and occupied with something out of my line of sight. Since he hadn't been having any "zipper" problems for a few days I was not quite as wary of him as I had been in the past. I half turned away from him as I leaned down to grasp the handle and lift the milk bucket. In a second he was beside me with his hands grasping me tightly just above each elbow. Milk sloshed over the side of the bucket as it dropped the couple of inches back down onto the milk stand. Why was he holding me so tightly, and what did he want quickly turned into vocal pleas for him to let me go, and finally into frantic, desperate, useless struggles to escape.

Life for me was never the same again. As he raped me physically, he not only took my innocence, self-worth, happy outlook and security, but he also managed to almost destroy forever my mental and emotional stability, and my trust in people. Before releasing me he threatened me with death if I told anyone what had taken place that morning.

Having been told once before that retribution would be swift and sure and knowing it would be by the Wangkai, I believed him also. Once released I tried to run in spite of the heaviness of the milk pail and its continual banging against my leg spilling the milk. After numerous checks over my shoulder I finally realized that he was not following me and slowed to a walk. Tears flowed down my face due to a mixture of pain, fright and anger. I remembered "as a Wangkai," which I felt I was, "it just wasn't the thing to cry." I had to stop for a bit to make sure my tears were all wiped away before I got home so no one would ask any questions. I sure didn't want to lie, but I really did not want to die. I realized how crafty he was to have chosen such a location. All physical evidence including our tracks in the dirt, which to me as a bush child was proof of what had happened, was erased as the goats raced and played in the pen.

I was a very ignorant and frightened young girl. Fear just seemed to overwhelm me in the days, weeks, and months that followed. Each new day I wondered to myself, was I a bad person, was I pregnant, and what had I done or not done that made him want to hurt me in this awful way.

At night I started having such terrifying nightmares that I hated to close my eyes in sleep for fear of the dreams that nightly haunted me; dreams filled with what had taken place, of never being able to escape and his threats of my death. The dreams only changed to additional nameless faces stalking and catching me. Even now some forty-five years later when I have had to relive that situation, such as for jury duty, or if during the day I feel vulnerable or threatened in some way the nightmares often will reoccur for about a week.

Life for me had changed in an instant from laughter and trust to anxiety and fear. If someone surprised me I no longer laughed, but jumped, and if really frightened, ran. If a white man I didn't know came too close to me, I became instantly frantic to be with people I knew, and if no one was close would run and hide. Finding and knowing where quick hiding places were, such as under Dad's huge desk, in the attic, and in my friendly bush became of paramount importance to me.

Once years later when sitting listening to some people reminiscing about old times and what happened to so and so; I suddenly could hardly breathe, for this man's name was mentioned. The person talking went on to say he had heard that the individual had gotten married and had two children. Another person piped up saying "Oh but his wife and kids died when their house burned down, but he escaped." Unkind thoughts raced through my head from "it should have been him," to "I wonder if he set the fire," and then "how unfair for him to escape while his family died."

I felt trapped by my overwhelming fears, and only felt safe and secure when in the bush, or with my stone-age tribal relatives. In a very vague subconscious sort of way I realized that something about me was different from the Aborigines; however, on the conscious level I saw no difference between us. While my face is white in color, I felt as if in my heart, core, or innermost being I was an Aboriginal. I was so like an Aboriginal child in my thinking, actions, activities and speech that I had been mistaken for an Aborigine more than once when a person heard, but did not see me in person.

In future years the following three realities, or truths, that I learned from the Aborigines, along with my faith in God as a result of my parents example and faith, would help me survive tough times.

The first reality or truth was that the Good God in heaven is good all of the time. They would never ever consider blaming Him for anything.

The second reality or truth was that the devil and his evil spirits are very present in our world today, and are always trying to influence people to do bad or evil things.

The third reality or truth was related to our God-given free will. Individuals make their own decisions and take action according to their own desires; therefore, each person is always responsible for their own actions.

Christmas & Creek

We lived in extreme poverty, but as children didn't know or care since all of us at Cundeelee lived at or near the same economic level. A couple of times we were recipients of what was called a missionary barrel. This was a container that usually came from overseas and could have interesting things in it, ranging from toys and clothes, to teabags or even a quilt. Sometimes receiving it seemed to be almost worse than getting nothing at all, especially for Mum.

Everything had to come through at least two sets of customs before reaching us and that alone took a huge toll on anything nice getting through. Reading the label of what was supposed to be in the box, was hard enough, but when people sent us their very well-worn castoffs and that was all that was left in the box, that was hard. If the items were sent in a tea chest (a box made of wood that at the beginning of its travels had housed tea), well that was something that could be used, and we were thankful for it. Once in a while a toy, dress, shirt, jacket, or even a quilt, which was in good condition, would survive customs for us to enjoy. Everything we had was always available to be given or shared with anyone, especially if they seemed to have a need that was more obvious or urgent than our own.

December and Christmas happen to come during summer time in Australia. In our part of the outback that meant dry and very hot weather. It was like Arizona's desert summer temperatures, with no cooling whatsoever. We had no electricity so there was no air conditioning, or even a fan to help cool us down. Dad and Mum tried to make Christmas a family day with an outdoor picnic, or a cool rather than a hot meal. In later years, when we lived in the house with the cement floor, we would sometimes just lay on the floor trying to get cool. When Christmas rolled around the first year we were at Cundeelee, Dad used a Eucalyptus tree as our Christmas tree.

Although it made no difference to Stephen or me, the others really missed having a "real" tree.

Sometimes it was in the small details that we saw God's loving hand had already been at work preparing something special just for us. Before the next Christmas had rolled around, Dad just happened to find, in the middle of nowhere, a small patch of real "Christmas Trees." In all of his travels this was the only patch he would ever find.

At Christmas we were delighted if we received a small toy of some kind, a few pieces of hard candy and an orange. For several years around Christmas time a kind person living on the coast sent numerous boxes of oranges to Cundeelee. They always made sure there were enough oranges for everyone. Since the people often suddenly went walkabout, a few times we each received more than one orange. We learned to like and enjoy the oranges, but not before making a mistake or two regarding how to eat them. The first time we received the oranges some of us had bitten into the skin and tasting the bitterness had thrown them in the ashes to cook. Dad had to show us how to peel and then eat them. Due to the lack of water, the "fruit" that grew wild in the Outback, was not naturally juicy so we were very surprised when we took our first bite. These "things" were not only drippy, but also very sticky. They became a special treat to look forward to each Christmas.

The men had lain sleepers across the width of our salt-river to make it easier for our vehicles to cross. The top, or crust, looked beautiful and crystal white with all of that dried salt; however, right under the surface lay black thick gumbo. Someone came up with a great idea. Dig a "swimming hole" about fifty feet away from the road, at the edge of the salt-river, and shore it up with sleepers. Come Christmas day, if we had water enough to spare for baths later, we could go swimming in this newly made salt pool. Actually, it wasn't really a swimming pool, more like a hole, since it was only two arm lengths from one side to the other. Being so hot out it was refreshing and fun to get wet and cool off. As long as everyone just hung on to the edge of the sleepers, and gently moved their feet all was well. The boys especially liked to jump, and kick, turning the water instantly into thick, black, muck. We'd wait about five minutes, after which most of the black goo would settle back down. Then, as gently as possible we'd try to clean up a bit as we continued our rare treat of being in water. I was told that this salt wash of ours was seven times saltier than the ocean. It sure stung our eyes when we got splashed, but it was great for helping to heal any sores we had if we could stand the painful stinging. At the end of the afternoon on Christmas day, we happily rode on back of the truck with our feet hanging over the edge. By the end of the five-mile ride the sun and the breeze had dried us into human crusts of black gumbo and salt crystals. Although we were tired, we now had to take a lot of time to clean up before we could have our "wash" and crawl into bed. No individual showers with as much time as we wished were waiting for us, but if I was lucky, a bath tub with the cleanest person going in and out first might just be me. Of course our clothes, which could now stand on their own, would have to soak for a few days, but all of this was Mum's gift of love to us at Christmas.

The day after Christmas was a British celebrated holiday called Boxing Day. I believe that originally the holiday was for boxing up food and items to share with your neighbors and people in need. Since all of our "boxes" had been shared on Christmas, we held a sports day. Later Dad added sack and three-legged races as well as dodge ball, but at first it was only games that related to the Aborigines' way of life. For the first sports day, competition was centered around who could run the fastest, jump the highest, throw and catch their returning boomerang, and accuracy plus distance in throwing a spear. Dad brought out an old tire he had saved that was good for nothing, but still capable of rolling. He then wedged a piece of a heavy cardboard into the opening of the tire, and made sure it was stuck in there straight and tight. The center of the cardboard was then blackened using half-burned cold coals. The man who threw his spear through this center mark while the tire was rolling, and from the furthest distance, won.

There were several ways in which the men rattled their spears. One sound meant a fight, another was a warning to stay clear of the area, and then there was show off time. I never saw them have so much fun and laugh so hard as on Boxing days.

When it came to the boomerang, there were two ways in which it could be thrown. One way was to throw it straightforward making it hit the ground, then jump up in the air in order to split open man or beast. If the intended object were missed, then another one would be thrown, while the first was returning to its owner. The other way to throw a boomerang could also be lethal, but it circled around in the air, before returning. It was only the second way of throwing, which was allowed at sports day, and even then accidents could happen.

One day early on, before the sports were too well organized, one fellow decided on the spur of the moment to throw his boomerang, and show Uncle Bob who was standing next to him, his new "good fella" boomerang. It really was a great flyer, but people shifted around a bit after he had thrown it, and he was not able to just reach out his hand and proudly catch it as he had intended.

Dad saw that if he didn't do something quickly a child was going to get hit in the head by the returning boomerang. Dad's reach was greater since he was so much taller than the boomerang's owner. In a split second, Dad reached out as far as he could putting his arm in front of the child's head taking the brunt of the heavy and fast returning wood. While the boomerang missed the child's head, it hit on the inside of Dad's arm near the elbow, and despite the fact that he was wearing his brown bomber's jacket, made a very nasty gash. Oh my, the fat was in the fire so to say. As Dad was holding his bleeding arm, he was also busy trying to prevent more blood shed, now on his behalf. Some had their spears ready to spear this fellow through the legs if Dad would just give them the "nod." Where a person was speared depended on the intent and severity of the crime or act committed against someone. Dad was instead, trying to explain to them that it was an accident, and he wanted them to lay down their weapons. The child was also in trouble for having been in the way, and not paying attention to his surroundings, which in turn had caused Uncle Bob to get hurt. My Dad was referred to as Mr. Stewart, Superintendent, and Bob, but the Aborigines seemed to prefer either "Tjamu" or "Uncle Bob." They had great reverence for him since he had shown them how much he cared about them, and also because he had come to tell them about the Good God who lived in the sky and His Son Jesus.

Punishment was always expected to be swift and sure for the guilty party. They did not believe in waiting for a jury trial for everyone had seen what had happened - so of course all spears were at the "ready." Forgiveness was only understood to take place after the offending party had received their just reward. Once Dad was sure there would be no more bloodshed due to the accident, he went and had someone stitch up his arm.

Never one to miss an opportunity, Dad put this story to good use in one of his Sunday morning lessons. It was interesting, for in their culture once the person in the wrong had been punished with some of his blood being shed, then forgiveness was attainable. Dad now had a way to explain to these stone-age people, the concept of how Jesus, being innocent, had bled and died for our wrongs so we could be forgiven and live eternally with the good God in heaven. Dad had been hurt, Jesus had died; both had bled for others and forgiven, nothing was required except to accept or reject their love gifts. The gift was free and could not be earned as it had already been paid for in blood. The story of Jesus was now understandable for they had seen an example of love in action.

At Christmas time when people looked at us in regards to gifts given and received or in pounds, shillings, and pence, of which we had few, we were rated well below the poverty level. In love of family and friends; however, regardless of skin coloring, we were exceedingly rich indeed.

I benefited greatly and learned much while living with the Aborigine peoples of Western Australia. So many nebulous as well as very distinct things I was taught by these people of the Outback would come back countless times in years to come, to help me cope with life and hang on regardless of my circumstances.

Nullabor Plain

Home

Breakdown

Home for a night

Nap Time

Hands Free

Church Service

Ready to eat

Pumping water from a rock hole

CANADA

An Outback Child, at Heart am I,
In culture and language, until I die.
Two cultures war now inside of me,
Each one wishing to be complete and free.

If I rise on the wings of the dawn, if I settle on the far side of the sea, even there your hand will guide me, your right hand will hold me fast. Psalms 139:9,10 (NIV)

Departure & Devils

The year was 1956 we had lived in Australia for six and a half years, I was now twelve and in eight months would become a teenager. I was secure in my tribe, and at home in my mind. Little did I realize that the winds of change were about to blow like a gale, tearing at the peace and stability of my very being. The time had come for us to leave the Outback and "go on furlough." This meant it was now time to report back to the individuals and churches overseas who were supporting us with both money and prayer. I remember Dad and Mum telling us to say good-bye to our "mates," that we could take one toy and to give the others away. The one toy that I chose to keep was the doll I had been given when I had my appendix removed.

Since I had heard Mum and Dad saying that we would be coming back, I too assured all of my Aboriginal friends that not only would I not forget them, but that it would not be long until I returned. Either my folks did not hear me saying this, or they decided to ignore it for the time being, but no one corrected or talked to me about it. We packed our few belongings, were driven the twenty-six miles to the railroad depot at Zanthus where we boarded the train for Sydney. The train journey across Australia is just remembered as a long trip with many stops, a blur of motion, noise, tiredness, and only Stephen and I speaking Wangatha.

Little did I know it would take me thirty-seven long years before I would see my Aboriginal friends or set foot once again on the soil at Cundeelee.

After we arrived and got settled in Sydney, a lady came up to me holding a string-like thing, which she proceeded to wrap around me in several places – definitely weird. The two new cotton dresses she made for me as a result though were beautiful to behold. One dress was pink and white checks while the other was blue and white. Being used to hand-me-downs, I felt very special to have two new dresses at the same time, and loved them for their bright colors and crisp texture.

The children in our family had been provided with socks and sandals since it was winter. The streets and surfaces we were now walking on ranged from cold and wet to very dirty. To me the sandals felt like lead weights on my feet. I thought that they were not only awkward and heavy, but also very noisy, after the near silent padding of bare feet I was used to hearing. In spite of it being winter it was still a daily struggle for me to remember to put on my sandals each morning. Since the footpaths were now manmade and comprised of hard surfaces, I felt as if I was losing a part of my identity for I could no longer "see" individual footprints and know who made them and where they went. Another bad thing about my sandals to my way of thinking was due to a habit I had learned in the bush, which I could no longer accomplish. I had become skilled at picking up whatever I wanted from the ground or floor by using my feet to feel and find the item, after which I would pick up the item with my toes. I had never had to do more than take a very quick glance downward, and my feet and toes did the rest. Rarely did I ever stoop over to pick up anything, especially nothing I could just pick up with my toes, in order to be on "the alert" to my constantly changing surroundings. Now however, if I dropped something I had to bend down for it, which to my way of thinking made me vulnerable. I now had to focus on the item rather than on what was going on around me plus I could not run easily from a crouched position.

Changes seemed to be happening almost every minute of the day, and nothing was normal anymore. I was bewildered and confused by the many new sounds, loud noise, crowds of people, and a strange language, not to mention the hustle and bustle of a city. While I did understand a little English, I was used to hearing it with Dad and Mum's American accent. This was pure "Aussie" English using slang and their own sayings.

My younger brother Stephen, having been born in the Outback was now six. Looking back I realize that Mum spoke English to Stephen and so he probably understood more than I at the time; however, I was older. Therefore I took it upon myself to not only explain things to Stephen, in Wangatha of course, but also not let him out of my sight. He was an independent little boy used to running wild. We were not used to seeing more than our two vehicles in a day or crowds of strange people, and certainly not used to being in a town, let alone a city. Stephen wanted to explore it all and I just wanted to hide.

In 1950 we had to have certain inoculations, before coming to Australia, and now we had to have more before leaving. When I got my shot in the arm I had on one of my new dresses. It was the beautiful, pink and white, pull-over-the-head dress with short puffy sleeves that ended in a two-inch wide band. During the day my arm started to ache, get hot, and swell up, but I never said anything for I was an Outback child and not used to complaining about small hurts. That night, when I tried to pull my dress over my head, I couldn't get my arm out of the sleeve, even with my sister helping. Mum came to say goodnight and seeing what had happened gave me a choice.

Either cut the band of the sleeve, which would forever mar my dress, or for me to wear the dress day and night until the swelling went down. I not only saw nothing wrong with wearing the dress for three days in a row, I also did not want my new dress ruined, so I choose the later. During the next several days Mum had to explain several times to people questioning her as to why my dress looked so wrinkled. I would always watch to see how their expression would change as Mum explained my situation. I wondered in silence what possible difference it could make to them what I wore. In my mind, with my limited Aussie English, I considered them to be "stickybeeks" a term used to describe a busybody or a nosy person.

Finally it was time for our big trip to America. I had no idea how long a trip it was nor how we would be traveling. I did not realize there was a huge ocean we would have to cross. We returned to America by boat because the fare was cheaper, and also because Mum and Dad thought we needed time to assimilate the many changes we were experiencing each day. It was unsettling and strange for nothing at all was familiar any longer.

We boarded the ocean-going British vessel the H.M.S. (His Majesties Ship) Oronsay in Sydney Australia for the first leg of our journey towards North America. Unfortunately for us, we sailed right into a hurricane, which lasted for three days. Dad and Darlene stayed topside as much as possible living on fresh air, soda crackers and ginger ale. Over half of the crew and most of the passengers including Mum, Dale, Stephen and I were throwing up or wishing we were dead. The sea was so rough we were in constant jeopardy of falling out of our bunks. It seemed as if all we did was roll from one side of the bunk to the other and back again.

Eventually, for our safety and after a few people had fallen out of their bunks injuring themselves, the three of us younger children were strapped down. They left Mum untied and on a lower bunk in case she needed to help us. Actually it was a great help to be strapped down. We had been using up an enormous amount of energy just trying to keep from rolling off of the bunk, and could now relax and rest a little between rolls and bouts of sickness.

Our first port or stop was Auckland, New Zealand where we were encouraged to get off the boat for a day of sightseeing. Having a small pocketbook and very little appetite, our family went to a nearby park to relax and get our land legs back. It was so lovely for the foliage all around varied in color only as to its shades of green. Here it was okay to sit on the lush grass. Birds of all types flew down checking to see if we had any handouts for them. A strange bird with a long bill and referred to as a Kiwi slowly and with patent unconcern foraged in and out of the shrubs near us.

Stephen and I thought it strange that no one tried to catch or kill any of the birds or small animals for a meal. Things had become so topsy-turvy we figured we had better ask Dad, before we went ahead and followed our normal behavior. Dad told us then that we could only catch and kill our own food at Cundeelee. To us it was just another black mark against this new alien environment.

All of our habits and survival instincts were suddenly becoming wrong. In spite of this new development we had a glorious day of freedom until it was time to make our way back aboard the ship.

I was fine until I reached the bottom of the gang-plank at which time I started to implore Mum and Dad in Wangkai, to not make me get on that thing again as it made my stomach hurt big time. It was very unlike me to make any kind of a scene. I was filled with dread, not wanting to be sick again and did not notice the purser come over. He wanted to know what the problem was and if he could help in any way. He had no idea of what I was saying, but he did know what kind of a three-day trip we had experienced and could sympathize with me. He promised me, via Dad, that all would be "good" now. The scene ended abruptly as Dad carried Marilyn up the ramp assuring her that her big time stomachache would not come back once we boarded, and said in the future to act like a big girl. I felt chastised, but not reassured.

Several sittings came and went before everyone felt well enough to return to the dining room for their meals. At Cundeelee we had learned from visiting government officials the "Aussie way" of eating food using a knife and fork, but at this table there were so many knives, forks and spoons. I kept sneaking quick glances at certain people to ascertain which utensils they used during each course of the meal. Stephen understood that I would show him, non-verbally of course, what to do, and he was to follow or mimic me throughout the meal. Except for the matter of eating, we did not open our mouths at the table. If we wanted something we tried to quietly signal one of our family members to meet our need, or we went without. I thought we were doing really very well at being almost invisible to the adults at our table in not bringing any attention to ourselves. The truth about pride and a fall was about to be realized up close and personal, by yours truly.

From time to time, I had noticed that one fellow on the other side and down the table from me kept glancing in my direction. His face seemed to indicate that there was something wrong with me. Finally his curiosity overcame him. I saw him look at me one more time, then lean over the table towards Dad. He rudely pointed at me with his knife and while waving his hand asked, "What is the matter with her, she never stops waving her hand over her plate?" It wasn't the words he said, for I didn't understand them; rather it was the look on his face as he leaned towards my Dad, and the pointing then waving motion of his hand, and I realized that I was either doing something that was questionable or at least strange. Dad looking down the table at me laughingly said, "well, she has been keeping flies away from her food for over six years, and it is so automatic she hasn't yet realized that there are no flies around here." Realization of what I was doing dawned the moment I saw his hand motions and I was totally mortified that I had been caught doing something wrong. I had been so intent on mimicking so as not to appear different from the people around me, I had instead brought attention to us by my very actions.

Someone then asked where we had lived, and while Dad talked I scanned the table checking for reactions in body language and facial expressions. Some looked at us as if we had suddenly become not good enough or contaminated in some way and could not wait to get away from our table. I didn't understand what was wrong, but I had experienced those looks before on deck, when someone overheard Stephen and me talking together. I felt as if I had shamed my family. For the rest of the trip there were fewer people at our table. I deliberately checked to see where they were now sitting to see what kind of people they thought "fit" them better. I was puzzled by their behavior for I was proud of my heritage and "my" people.

I decided I had better try even harder to be like the Mountain Devil, which was a lizard we had in the Outback. It changed its color to match the color of whatever it was on, so as not to be noticed. I was starting to think that my survival in this strange New World would depend upon my ability to copy while remaining invisible until I was able to blend in with this new environment completely. This meant mimicking everything until there was nothing I did or said that would attract attention to me as being different from those around. I soon figured out that as long as I did not open my mouth I could fool anyone. The lizard remained a lizard regardless of its coloring, which was only a trick used to stay alive. I determined that from now on, regardless of my surroundings, I would do my best to melt into the background. But in my heart and mind I determined to stay a child of the outback until I could return home to my people and Cundeelee.

The H.M.S. Oronsay's next stop was the Fijian Islands, and Suva in particular. This time when the announcement came that we were docking, I was one of many on deck peering down through the railings. It was so far down that I had to strain to hear the welcoming band and see the people on a tiny little platform. I worried about the people for I thought the jetty would be crushed for sure since the ship was so large. Sighting a Fijian created a burst of excitement within me as I thought, for a few brief seconds, that I was seeing an Aborigine. It was their dark skin only for they sported lovely huge hairdos. Their hair was kinky, dark and thick standing out in a complete circle about six inches long around their entire head. The policemen wore dark blue/black tunic tops with a white sash across it, and mid-calf-length, white, wrap-around-skirt, with pointed edges. As we talked to one friendly Fijian, he stuck a pencil into his thick bushy hair until it disappeared. Watching our eyes widen, he told us (fib or not I don't know) that he had lost several pencils that way, and he'd have to wait until he combed his hair in a week or so, before he'd to be able to find them again.

Boarding time seemed to come around so fast, but now I gritted my teeth, and in spite of a churning stomach mimicked everyone else by appearing to have no fear of returning to the ship.

I was becoming a good little actress at hiding my real feelings behind a mask of uncaring compliance.

There was a playroom on the boat where just kids could play, but Stephen and I didn't know what anyone was saying, nor did we know how to play their games, and since we seemed to make people nervous we rarely played there. We just did not fit in; therefore, we spent a lot of time just listening and watching people walking, swimming, playing deck coits etc., the latter of which we tried when no one else was around. We thought that most of the people on board exhibited very strange behavior, so to amuse ourselves made up stories about them. All the while I desperately wished to be back home in the surroundings of my familiar Outback.

One stretch of ocean seemed never to end for we were six days without seeing any land. We did see flying fish and sea birds, but that did not compensate for solid land. I was beginning to worry about not being able to ever see or touch my feet to the wonderful thing called earth, dirt, or ground. My memories thus far concerning travel had for me been almost exclusively by my own feet on the unmoving security of mother earth.

In my culture questions were rarely asked, so once again I gritted my teeth and passively waited for either land or the next surprise to materialize.

It was during this time that I remember Dad and Mum telling us that we were going to see our relatives, and they showed us some funny money called dollars. Having not used or needed money at Cundeelee, for there were still no stores of any kind out there, and not understanding what they were trying to explain to me, I ignored all but the word relatives. Now relatives to me meant my Aboriginal relatives, so I reasoned that we must be headed back to Cundeelee. This to me was great and welcome news, for as far as I was concerned this trip was long over-due to end. The people I had encountered on this trip were rude, the noise was never-ending, and there was hardly any food with which I was familiar or thought tasted good. Being used to living with a people who went walkabout all of the time, and always came back to where they had started out from, I naturally assumed we were doing the same thing.

Life for about two months had been interesting and exciting, but very exhausting, for I was constantly on the alert now for "bad men" and we were in crowds of people every day. I was a very shy, quiet child to begin with and used to my mostly peaceful, beautiful Outback. Not only was the noise appalling, it masked the sound of footsteps.

One day the captain announced over the loud speaker that in a few days we would cross the Equator. This event would be celebrated by a party and would be referred to as the "Captain's Ball." It was to be a costume or masquerade party in which the three people who were judged to have the most creative or best costume would each receive a prize. For days we saw people scurrying around the decks carrying items bundled tightly in their arms to prevent others glimpsing their treasures. They seemed to be very excited and happy for they laughed as they hurried along the decks.

Neptune, the god of the sea, came up out of the sea – though I was sure I'd seen this apparition come from the swimming pool. He appeared to be about seven feet tall and as he walked his robe, which shimmered like silver painted with blue and green streaks, trailed on the deck behind him. Seaweed hung from his crown, shoulders and pitchfork. He was an awesome, and to us, a fearful sight. We were not allowed to get close to him, and he disappeared after going to see the captain. Having lived with a superstitious race that spoke of devils and spirits all day long I had no trouble believing that we had been visited be the god of the sea.

The costume party was to take place after supper so the children could enjoy the show before going to bed. The real, or adult party, would begin after the children had been bedded down.

My sister Darlene at seventeen was very shy and truly wished just to be left alone, but some women on board "knew" better. They decided to take a hand and the night of the ball they arrived enforce. First a kind of stain was applied to her face and hands, a wig placed on her head, and with a lovely colored blanket thrown over her shoulders she was pronounced ready for the party. She was now an unwilling Indian Princess on route to a costume party. I was curious, but baffled over the paint since the only time I'd seen people paint their faces was when there was a special sort of ceremony going on in or near the camp. Paintings on one's body in my tribe signified some special ritual, dance or witchcraft was going to take place, which often resulted in blood being shed.

About five rows of chairs had been set up on deck for spectators to sit while enjoying the contestants' parade by in their diverse attire. At first the line of hopeful contestants was so long that it snaked down the deck and out of sight around a far corner. On the second round, after the first pass was completed, the judges started pulling out their first round choices. On the first pass I had been horrified to see not one, but three costumed red devils complete with horns and tail. In the culture that I had grown up in, one thing you didn't do was mess with evil spirits. While I thought about their lack of good sense and their daring, I determined to stay as far away from them as I possibly could. The judges finally reduced their choices down to twelve, with Darlene and one of the red devils that I had really bad vibes about, still in contention for a prize. Dad and Mum had taken Stephen down to bed, but I had asked if it was okay if I sat and waited for Darlene. I was sitting in the third row from the front. Looking around I was surprised to see that most of the fold-up chairs near me were now vacant. I did not like being so close and vulnerable to things I did not understand - especially the red devil since I couldn't see his face. It was very noisy with people wanting the show to be over, others still having fun and pointing out their favorites, while contestants tried last minute poses to attract and hopefully help the judges decide in their favor. The judges were undecided as to the three finalists. I think the fellow in the red devil costume sensed my fear and decided to aid his "devil antics" to procure a win. I was sure, due to his mannerisms, and even though I couldn't see his face, that he was the rude fellow who had been at our table. When I saw him start towards me I slipped back another row, trying to keep an eye on him, while at the same time find an escape route. At first I tried to escape without attracting any attention. I did not move fast enough for he was able to reach out and grab one of my arms. He then half-pulled half-dragged me behind him. I tried to either grab or push over each chair we passed. I had decided that I would not go with him quietly, and hoped that the sounds of the chairs crashing on the deck would make him stop. All the time he was dragging me along he was laughing like a demented person. I was simply terrified and even convinced that an evil devil and not just a man had me in tow. We were just clearing the first row of chairs, with him still dragging me along, when a person in uniform came by and told him to let me go, adding didn't he see that he was scaring me to death. I was so shaken and scared by what had occurred, that I never took in whether Darlene won a prize, or if I even waited for Darlene before racing down flight after flight of stairs into the bowels of the ship to the safety of our cabin.

That night old memories merged with new ones of not being able to escape, and terrifyingly real nightmares haunted my sleep for the rest of the trip. I remained on such an exhausting "high alert" of any male looking the least bit suspicious, that I simply do not remember the rest of the voyage.

The next thing I consciously remember was being in Seattle at Grandpa and Grandma's place, and the smell of his pipe. The smoke curling up from it reminded me of a far away land, where the Aborigines used smoke signals, and I wished they could see and answer one from so far away.

Rain & Relatives

It wasn't long before I was noticing my dismal surroundings with puzzlement and dismay. I saw strange trees and not very many pretty birds, and wondered what had happened to the sun. Noise was never-ending, whether one was inside or outside, and it seemed to me that almost everything here was made to create or make some kind of noise. So many things were made out of metal and moved, and were categorized as definitely spooky by my standards. For instance, when we went into a store, we went into a small room called a lift, which as soon as the door closed started to move so fast that I thought my stomach had left my body. I embarrassed everyone with me by sinking to the floor and curling up in a ball until all movement had stopped. Mum showed me by using one word and a motion (the Wangkai way) that next time I was to hold the rail and to stand very still. Then there was the escalator that, just as I would try to put my foot on it, moved, making me jump back in fright as I watched it change shape and grow. Spooky!

Rain, rain, rain; no more sandals, must wear shoes to keep my feet dry. Mum took me downtown via a bus to a shoe store to get me some appropriate footwear. I had never seen so many shoes in all my life. There was a strange "devil" machine, which after I tried on a new shoe, I was instructed to put my foot into to check for "fit." Looking into the machine I thought it had turned my foot into just bones. I tried on many shoes, which in those days all had hard uppers or tops, and hurt my toes. Each time I placed my foot into the machine I was afraid the next time I pulled my foot out it would just be bones and stay that way. Finally Mum and the salesman gave up trying to find a pair about which I didn't complain. They picked out a pair for me and said these are wide and long enough; wear them. It was a very unnerving day for me, from our arrival to our departure.

Footpaths were now to be called sidewalks, and made out of a cold hard material which showed no footprints. A footpath made sense, being a path for feet to walk on, but what did a sidewalk mean? A wireless became a radio, a torch was a flashlight, petrol was now gas, and a biscuit a cookie. No more morning and afternoon billy tea breaks, where everyone sat down for a bit in the shade of a tree, put a can of water with tea leaves in it on the fire, and chatted until the tea was ready. There was water inside the homes. All I had to do was turn on the tap, and there was both hot and cold water; no more boiling it for fifteen minutes before I was allowed to drink it. I had learned that there were twelve pennies to a shilling, and twelve inches to a foot. A shilling and a quarter were about the same size and had two silver coins smaller, but now a quarter was twenty-five cents, but twelve inches still made a foot. How was I supposed to know what changed and what stayed the same – was there some sort of hidden rule? A real kicker though was due to the toilet, bathtub and sink all being located in the same room – totally gross.

There were no lanterns, but just a flip of a switch made the lights glow. I watched as an adult turned a knob on a radio, and expected to hear the Flying Doctor or someone like him talk. It was a shock to learn that radios over here weren't much good at all for they were only good for listening. There was a box on the wall with a crank called a telephone that they used to call the doctor or just to talk to someone for no important reason at all, and it stayed working all night.

And then there was a big box with a glass front that sat in the living room of my Grandparents home that had Stephen and me mystified and quite spooked. It was called a television. After my Grandma would go over and do something, the box would light up and soon there would be people walking, talking, even dancing and singing inside it. We were curious so, when no one was in the room with us, we checked the box out thoroughly by looking behind and underneath it. We were trying to find out where the little people lived, and if we could spot them. In our minds they had to be little people to be able to fit in the box yet look like full-grown adults. For days we stalked that box trying to catch the little people coming or going and wondered where and when they ate and slept. We wondered if they lived their whole lives in the box, if they ever tried to escape, and how so many lived in one tiny box. We watched to see if anyone put any food near the box for them. Since we didn't understand anything about these little people, we spent a lot of time worrying over the unfairness of how they had to work every time the box lit up. We asked no questions in accordance with "our" culture, but watched and waited to see how the adults were handling the situation.

We had never seen or been to a movie theater. At first the Aborigines believed that if their picture was taken their spirit was captured in the box that was pointed at them. In later years the bolder ones allowed their face to be "captured," and marveled at seeing their friends faces in photos. Not having mirrors they did not recognize their own face.

We even wondered vaguely if it was spirits in the box, but decided that it couldn't be since Dad and Mum allowed us to watch it. When we finally realized that no one seemed to care about the people in the box, we decided to accept this mystery and move on to finding out if we would be allowed to bring them to life.

I longed for my peaceful Outback. I missed hearing the breeze as it touched the leaves of the gum trees making them whisper, of small animals scurrying here and there, people talking in "my" language and only once in a while the noise of a vehicle. I hadn't known I had lived in such a quiet, isolated, secluded, unique place or that such continual noise could and did exist.

My nose, which had enjoyed sniffing the air, and knowing each smell, now seemed to be only good as an appendage on my face, since I could no longer classify anything.

My eyes were kept busy trying to memorize faces, keep an eye out for questionable people, figure out what was acceptable behavior here, so I could copy it, and watch my folks to see how they responded to each new and strange happening.

My eyes and ears were constantly busy, taking in my surroundings as I watched people and listened to the conversations buzzing around me. I kept alert just in case what was being said applied to me in some way. When a person did talk to me, their accent and words were so strange that the little English I did know often did not seem to match up with what I thought they might have said.

I soon realized since I would sit almost motionless for a long time, that the adults tended to forget I was there and carry on their conversations as if I was not present. I overheard conversations from time to time about our family having gone overseas, and how unhappy that had made some of our relatives. Body language, facial expressions, and tone of voice were things to which I was used to paying a great deal of attention. In this way I learned more about real feelings and attitudes than the adults often realized.

Some of our relatives questioned Dad and Mum repeatedly as to why we couldn't stay in the USA and serve the Lord here. I saw in their body language, as well as the tone of voice, their frustration and lack of understanding for they loved and missed our family. They simply did not understand my parents' need to obey God's direction or Dad and Mum's love for the "pagan" Aborigines.

Classes & Cold

It wasn't long until once again we were all packed and ready to go "walkabout." This meant a road trip, with many stops, to speak in Churches and stay in unknown people's homes. At the meetings Dad usually spoke and showed some slides and then we kids would sing or speak in Wangatha.

Our ultimate destination was a small town in Alberta, Canada. My folks had written to the school explaining where we were coming from, that we were traveling, and would be arriving about two months late for the start of the 1956 fall term.

We had just come from winter, no snow of course, and here we were going into winter again, but nothing like I had ever known. It was time to get us children into school since the fall school term was already long under way.

The first day Dad drove me the two or so miles to enter me formally into first grade. Ever after, unless there was a blizzard, we walked. We first went to "The Principal's" office where a formidable-looking lady greeted us. From there, the three of us proceeded down the hall and up the stairs to the correct classroom where I was introduced to the class as the child from Australia.

Miss Gale, the teacher of the sixth grade class, having been earlier apprised of my situation had tried to prepare her students for my arrival by having a history lesson on the Aborigines and Australia. Unbeknown to me, the students had missed the fact that I was a missionary child and white; hence they expected me to be a full-blooded dark-in-color Aborigine from Australia.

Well, as I stood there by the door between my Dad and my new teacher, they just sat and stared at me. One boy finally piped up and said "she's not an Aborigine," and with those words said, I became an outcast, or so it seemed. They had been excited and ready for the novelty of having a real live Australian Aborigine in their class. Instead they had gotten a small waif of a white girl, who's outward appearance seemed no different from any other small white girl in their classroom.

For a long time only one girl in my class, a farm girl by the name of Dorothy, who rode the bus to school, would speak to or with me. To me it seemed as if I'd entered a very cold place. There was not only the cold weather outside, but also the coldness generated by many types of segregated groups within our all "white" classroom. The first segregation of course was boy versus girl, then rich farm children versus poor farm children. There were the children from a special home that was only for missionary children with parents in China, and finally there were the children of the staff members who worked for the school. It was here that I would learn that I did not "fit" in any group.

Since we lived so far from school we took a lunch just like the farm children who rode the bus, and as a result, over lunches, Dorothy and I became good friends. Dorothy not only became a friend she also became my main source of information, and as the years went by taught me how to do things "correctly" in this new culture.

Girls, regardless of their age, were required to wear dresses or skirts; however, when it got really cold we were allowed to wear heavy leggings or ski pants under our skirt or dress. Many a winter's morning it felt as if I was too bundled up to walk, let alone run if the need arose. Sometimes when we were walking we were so bundled up that all that was visible to tell one from another would be our eyes. My face would be so cold with my cheeks feeling like lumps of ice. It even hurt to talk until I'd been inside for a while. I did at times enjoy the snow, and being bundled up enough to stay warm, but I kept feeling like a butterfly that had gone backwards, from being light and free, to being bound up in a tight cocoon by clothes, rules, and weather. I had to wear goulashes over my shoes to keep my feet dry, but I detested their bulk and weight. I did love to hear the crunch of the snow under foot, and would stomp along with the others, which helped to relieve some of my intense, but well hidden and tightly bottled up feelings.

Christmas was beautiful with a blue sky and snow, but oh, so cold, and so unlike past Christmas days of over 100 degrees, bare feet, and swimming. I was homesick for my friends, but content since I was with my family and we were having fun playing or learning to play simple board games.

School was a daily nightmare as I struggled to figure out what the teacher was saying. Did she want us to do something or were we just to listen? I was forever glancing around the room to see the kids reactions such as grabbing a book, only to close it and get another, etc. The students in my class couldn't figure out why I didn't know English - after all I had white skin. Miss Gale, soon realized how very far behind everyone I was, and that I was lacking many of the basic fundamentals. I was having trouble with math, for the few sums I'd ever done had been in pounds, shilling, and pence. This new money didn't have any meaning for me since I had none of my own, never went shopping, and it had been less than three months since I had seen my first nickel, dime, or quarter.

The Australian expressions and slang I did know were not understood, so I tried very hard to copy the way others talked in order to be "invisible." Stephen and I continued to speak Wangatha at home, for it was the language that we both thought in, and after a hard day, speaking in "our language" gave our brains a rest. Each day after school I talked with Stephen trying to help him understand this "New World" we were experiencing. I did not understand it, but the little I learned I passed on to him – not that he always wanted to learn "my lessons." I did not want him to have to experience the pain I was going through each day of seeming to be the stupidest person in the classroom. I was so busy learning to copy what and how people did things that I became everyone but me. Mum always said that I should have become a teacher, since up until this time I could often be found explaining something I had learned to someone else. What Mum didn't realize was I stopped having anyone to communicate with when Stephen returned to Australia. It was at this time I ceased to "teach or help others" for I was the one badly in need of help.

Each and every week we were to learn one Bible verse. The teacher always picked it out herself and would slowly read it out loud. She would tell us why she had picked out that particular verse, explain the meaning of the larger words, and how we could apply its meaning to the way we lived each day. Next she printed the verse on the blackboard, and then had us read it out loud with her as she pointed to each word. Each day for a week we would slowly read the assigned verse from the blackboard. As I began to hear the sound and see the spelling of a word at the same time, I started to learn to speak and spell English words by memorizing them.

During school hours I felt caged, panicky, stupid, lost, and most of all totally bewildered. I didn't understand most of what was going on so I would hardly talk to anyone, but I was always alert, watching, and listening. Since I could hardly read, I compensated by becoming excellent at quoting whatever I heard. What no one seemed to realize was that I rarely knew the meaning of what I had quoted, and in reality all I had done was show that I was paying attention.

There were so many words in the English language that sounded exactly the same, but had a different meaning and spelling. It was very confusing. In "my" language, words had their own meaning, but one needed to listen for a tone or slight inflection to be able to tell the difference between words. I kept listening when people talked and could not hear any change in their tone of voice, so how could I know that flour and flower were spelled differently. If questions put to me required only a yes or no answer, or were simple then I would nod or shake my head. The longer the question, the longer it took me to figure out the meaning of the question, the English words I would need to use, and how I thought the person wanted me to respond. One thing that I had noticed was how much people talked and how little of it was information. Also when people talked no one seemed to watch anyone for a response. They either cut in talking or turned to talk to someone else. Why, "back home" I could carry on an entire conversation using only gestures or gestures with one or two words. The other person would respond in the same manner, and then the conversation was through. If I asked a question, it was never okay to turn away before the person had answered it. I could hardly wait to go "home."

Spring finally arrived with lovely lilac-colored crocuses pushing up through the ice and snow, and then it was summer vacation. What a relief to be out of school for several months.

The summer of 1957, a kind and generous person gave our whole family the gift of a week's lodging in a cabin at Pine Lake. The cabin was large with weather-beaten siding, a screened-in porch, and was shaded by trees. It was such fun to run and play amongst trees again. I had really missed them since we now lived on the flat, wind-swept prairies. Dad loved to fish, and since he rarely got a chance, this was relaxation at its best, for there was even a rowboat to complete the deal. He always liked to go fishing really early in the morning, and if we weren't ready, he would go without us. One particular morning I was up, dressed, and ready to go, but Stephen was still asleep when we left to go on the lake. Now fishing to Dad was serious business, and that meant no talking, rocking the boat, or even reading a book - just fishing. I didn't mind sitting for a while, but after an hour or two was a little weary, besides which I was always more interested in what was going on around the lake, on the shore etc. than in catching anything. I had noticed a small figure in a boat on the far side of the lake, tugging at the oars with a sort of hit and miss, in and out of the water. As I kept watching I thought - I know that kid. It was my seven-year-old, brother, Stephen. At the same time I realized that he did not know how to swim, and that he was not wearing a life jacket. Stephen, having finally spotted us, was heading albeit erratically, in our direction. Since he had already covered so much of the lake searching for us, and since the lake was really calm, I kept an eye on him without alerting Dad. Stephen timed his arrival well as Dad had just caught, and was still dealing with; a very large nasty looking fish called a pike. I fully expected Dad to scold him, but Stephen immediately started yelling why hadn't we waited for him, as he had wanted to go fishing with us. I couldn't believe it but it worked, for other than having to row himself to shore ahead of us, he was not even punished in any way, well, other than the blisters on his hands. Oh how I wished to have been born a boy, or even the baby, for either seemed much better than my life.

It never once entered my thoughts, since no one talked about it, but the three of us older children were going to be staying in Canada when Dad, Mum, and Stephen returned to Australia. All of this time I had just sort of existed by taking a day at a time as children do, just waiting for the year to be over when we would be heading back to Australia and my friends. I could hardly wait to get back to the place in which I wasn't a misfit, was never so cold, and understood not only what was said, but also things happening around me. In my mind I clung tenaciously to Wangatha, thinking in that dialect first and then translating the words I could into English. No one realized the daily struggles I faced for I was a very shy, quiet and reserved child, who did not talk very much. I don't think my parents had even a glimmer of an idea of how awful this life was for me, and how my whole focus was survival until I was able to go back "home." It was my complete unawareness of reality and lack of understanding that would make my situation so incomprehensible to me for so long a period of time. I had been well taught by the Aborigines to accept and cope with unexpected situations, not to grissle (complain), or ask why, but to do the best I could to make it through an ordeal in one piece. I was about to find out how good my indoctrination had been.

Deserted & Dorm

During the winter of 1956 and the spring of 1957 Dad drove a big coal truck delivering coal to homes in town and the surrounding area. In the spring and summer of 1957 he worked for a farmer, the father of one of my classmates. From time to time Dad, or we as a family, would go to churches or homes to tell about the work amongst the Aborigines of Australia. Dad would tell stories about our life in the Outback, what God was doing in the lives of some of the Aborigines, and a few of the miracles that had taken place. If we were along we children would sing or talk in Wangatha, and after questions had been answered, whether it was at a church, or in a home, we usually ended up having a meal before heading homeward. Each time Dad spoke it made me more anxious to get back home.

One day we went to a home having been invited for the evening meal, but there was a strange feeling in the air and they didn't once ask about Australia. There was a large man with his very thin tired looking wife, and six children under twelve. The youngest was just a small baby, who appeared to be a pale blue in color and just lay very still in its cot. I remember hearing the people say that "she" would have duties, and being the eldest at thirteen, would have to look after the younger children, as well as with the housework. I remember thinking that I was thirteen, and wondered who and what they were talking about. I had not been able to make any sense of the whole evening's conversation so dismissed it completely from my mind.

A few days later we went to another home for a delicious meal. This family was made up of a very nice looking couple, who had two sons, and a cute wee daughter. The children were all younger than I was and my quick assessment was that the older son seemed very pale and quiet, while the younger boy looked like he thrived on mischief. They all seemed very happy together, and we talked some about Australia. I had been silent and polite as usual, and heard no strange conversations so went happily to sleep that night knowing it was only a matter of days before we would be headed back home to Australia.

The packing was all done. I was more than ready to go back to my friends and language, the climate where I didn't have to wear shoes, the food that tasted good, and where I could hunt for my own snacks if and when I wished. My home of colorful birds, red dirt, graceful gum trees, spinifex, Aborigines, billy tea, damper, and kangaroos beckoned me.

Darlene and Dale were in High School, so they were old enough to live in the dorms, but I was too young, so of course it never once entered my mind to think I wasn't headed back to Cundeelee. I was now in seventh grade, but to be able to stay in the dorm you had to be in ninth grade. The dorms for the high school boys and girls were quite a distance apart, and had a number of buildings between them, helping to insure that there would be no socializing between the sexes. All of the classrooms, even in the grade school, had a two to three foot space down the center of the room with the boys on one side, and the girls on the other. I did not mind that in the least, and as far as I was concerned the farther away that the boys were, the better my stomach felt. At that time there were a lot of high school students being sent to this particular boarding school who's only alternative was a reformatory or jail. It was a very strict school and there were lots of rules, due in part to tough kids needing to experience structure and discipline in their lives.

I have skipped ahead a bit.

The next thing that happened came as a great shock, and although it was for my long-term good educationally, for years to come it left me with many emotional scars. Reliving that time brings back some very painful memories. It is hard to write about how much fear, anguish, and grief at being so far from her own family, there was in one small, scared, thirteen-year-old girl. It was caused in part to my lack of understanding the English language, and my parents' lack in the Wangatha dialect. The night before we were to leave and head for Australia, my parents sat me down and tried (so I have been told, but don't remember) to tell me that I was going to be staying in Canada. I hadn't the slightest idea that they were leaving me, for good, with the second family we had visited.

The Wangatha language had only a limited vocabulary. For instance, numbers only went as high as three. If someone was to say "sit down and wait," it was the way it was said that determined whether time was to be measured in minutes or hours. There was no way to explain to me how many minutes, days, weeks, months, or even years were being talked about, and yes, it was in years that the time would be measured.

I remember it was a cold, crisp morning and my things had been moved to this home, but we often stayed in various homes when we were traveling. I just didn't notice in all my excitement to be "going home" that only my bags were there. That morning I had walked to school, now less than a mile, with the kids and returned with them to the house for lunch. Dad, Mum and Stephen had lunch with us, then said that they would be on their way. I figured they were headed for another meeting, and they'd pick me up after school was out, but I wanted go with them now. We walked out the door and down the stairs to the sidewalk, to be overwhelmed by adults crowding around us talking and taking pictures. The adults just wouldn't leave off talking to Mum and Dad, and since I was a polite child, I soon stood on the fringes of the crowd waiting for a chance to talk to them myself. I finally had to leave or be late for school, and so in frustration and a little puzzled over the adults' behavior, I turned abruptly on my heel and alternating between walking and running arrived back at school just before the late bell rang.

At recess that afternoon some of the kids in my class told me that my parents were gone, and that they had left me on purpose, but I told them I was leaving in a day or two for Australia. The next day I had some adults stop me to say that they had personally "waved my folks out of town" at about five the previous afternoon. I couldn't believe it. It just couldn't possibly be true! I couldn't even talk to my older sister or brother, because at that time I had no idea where they were staying, or even if they were also with Mum and Dad. In one day I had lost my entire family, my hopes and dreams, with nary a hug, kiss or even a good-bye.

I was heart and home sick, consumed by thoughts that everyone had abandoned me, and that there was nothing I could do about it. I became totally focused on my own situation and for a while gave no thought for anyone except myself. Lessons learned in my "old culture" now helped me to wait unquestioning, but not without worrying, about the possible reasons for my being left behind. It preyed on my mind that maybe if I were good enough I would either be sent for or they would return to pick me up. I would wait and see. I would continue to practice speaking the Wangatha language in my head and never, ever forget it.

Dad and Mum had many stops and a lot of time between leaving me, and arriving in the Outback of Australia. As long as the stamp on their infrequent letters was not from Australia, I retained high hopes, and never doubted that I was returning to Australia with them.

Most people around me thought that because I was being good, and was quiet, I was coping very well and understood this separation from my family.

I did not.

I decided that I would not bring shame on my family or my people by crying, but neither would I, from henceforth, like anyone too well in case they also disappeared without leaving tracks I knew how to follow.

I became little Miss Independence, aloof but always listening, silent but carefully watchful.

I did not want to feel the slightest touch of another human, for I felt if anyone touched me, that I would shatter into a million tiny irretrievable pieces.

Announcement & Adopted

The compassionate Thompson family who had taken in this "Child of the Outback" was made up of John and Betty (called Uncle and Aunt to this day), Calvin or Cal, Douglas or Doug, and Kathy. Years later I found out from Aunt Betty that there had been an announcement made in the tabernacle about a child, a girl, who needed a place to stay when her missionary parents returned to Australia. Aunt Betty said that when she heard the announcement it was as if the Lord was asking her if she would be willing to take this child into her home and life. She was a young woman with a husband and three young children who did not know my family or me, and yet her answer was "yes, Lord, I would be willing." Nothing came of it for many long months, until the day when her long-ago "yes," turned into "Marilyn, welcome to our home and family."

> How do you mold, an Outback child -
>
> Who is used to bare feet, and running wild -
>
> Gum trees, roo's, and spears that fly -
>
> To shoes, and snow, and the forever why?

The summer of 1998, I made a long overdue visit to see Aunt Betty and Uncle John and he mentioned witnessing my leaving for school. He said he had marveled at my strength of character and being able to just leave without making a fuss. He had always wondered if he would ever have been that strong in a similar situation. Now that he knows the real story his whole perspective of the scene he thought he had witnessed took on a completely different perspective.

Everyone always seemed to know more about what was going on than I regarding my situation. I was lonely, in shock, scared and very homesick. I had been looking forward so much to having a proper breakfast with vegemite on my toast, Sunshine powdered whole milk on my weetabix, and milo to drink. I missed the smell and taste of Karlkurla, damper with golden syrup, billy tea, kangaroo meat, and that just started my list. I missed the familiar Aussie words such as Ta, Bloke, Chooks, Jumper, Sheila, Ute, and that list went on and on also.

I was asked by Aunt Betty to help her hang clothes on the line and to bring the clothes pins. I wondered what she wanted a small, sharp metal pin for. I quickly learned that my "pegs" were her "clothespins." Two questions continually came and went in my head. Will I ever be able to understand what people say and really mean, and when are my parents coming for me? While language difficulties kept me listening, emotional stress kept me alert and mistrustful of almost everyone. I was trying so very hard to be patient and good so I could go home to the Outback. With my limited understanding, I figured that being obedient had helped me get home the time I went to the hospital and had to stay with a strange family, so maybe that was what was needed again.

Little Miss Big Ears heard adults talking amongst themselves about children who had caused their parents to have to return, and what a shame that was for the family. I figured this out to mean that if I was bad I would bring shame to my parents who would have to return to Canada to get me, but that because of me being bad they would not be allowed to return to Australia. I wouldn't dare be bad, for what would happen to me if these kind people decided not to look after me – I just had to be good until my folks came for me.

As the days, then months, continued to mount, I finally began to realize that I was going to be left with these people for quite a long time - like maybe forever even. It wasn't that I had anything against the family I was with, for I liked them very much. They just weren't my family, and I just could not begin to find a reason for having been left here with them. It wasn't until I was shown, by use of a globe, where Australia and my parents were that it started to become real. I understood even better how very dependent I was on the goodness and mercy of this family for my folks were over ten thousand miles away.

Little did I know that it would be more than four long years before I would again see their faces or hear their voices. It gave me little comfort to know that in an emergency a cable could be sent to them via their short-wave radio. I also knew that I was going to have to rely totally on their letters to communicate their location, their health and their love for me.

It was only with special permission, and then not every Sunday afternoon, that I was allowed to visit with my sister and brother in the huge dining room for a couple of hours. Each sister and brother group sat at a different table, too far away from the person monitoring us to hear what was said, but with our hands in view of them to keep us from passing notes to or from other people. It was not exactly an exciting family get together. I was never allowed to visit them in their dorms, and they were only rarely allowed to visit the home in which I was living.

A classmate of mine had been adopted soon after her birth. I didn't know what adopted meant until my friend told me that it was a "throw away" or abandoned child. This individual had been left on a doorstep as an infant. This was a new thought and started me thinking a lot about the possibility of my being a "throw away" child. Maybe this was the reason for my being left at different times, the latest being with the Thompson family. I didn't think I was going to be adopted by them, for I still heard from my parents. It was so very confusing. I next started contemplating the ways in which I thought I was different from the other members in my family. My list began with my ability to speak the Wangatha language the best, although Stephen was now almost equal in my opinion. My list continued with the color of my hair and eyes, and ended up with my short stature for I was the shortest person in our family. Without ever discussing it with anyone, I had now sorted it out to my satisfaction, that the reason I had been left in Canada was due to the fact that I was adopted.

After reaching this conclusion I proceeded to make two resolutions. The first was to never ever forget my Wangkai language, relatives and friends. The second was to survive regardless of what it took until I could get back home to the Australian Outback and my people.

Cage & Cars

It was a tough new situation for all of us, but especially for Aunt Betty and me, as we struggled with everyday living from extremely different perspectives, and with little ability to communicate. She, I found out years later, had no idea that the child she was taking into her home spoke very little English. She had not done any research into my family, background or upbringing. At this time she also shared with me, that at times she thought I looked angry, but that I had been a very quiet and shy child. She had no idea that until the day that I was left with them I had rarely spoken English at home, and was far from fluent in it.

Things that were perfectly natural and normal to her were foreign to me. Let us take the matter of washing dishes, or better yet, my hair. To me all of the water, which was being wasted by just going down the sink, and not recycled in some way was simply horrific. So much waste by letting the water run until the water got hot, instead of just boiling some to use. Why should I want to waste water by washing my hair more than once a month, or at the most once a week? At Cundeelee, due to the lack of water, we had only been able to have a bath, with several using the same water of course, once a month. Each night, in an effort to keep the sheets clean as long as possible, we washed our feet one person at a time using a common basin and the same water. I grew up knowing our water supply was limited, and therefore very precious. Running out of water was a continual, serious hazard we endured, which taught us to be extremely careful not to waste it. The letters from Mum and Dad would usually include, "please pray for rain, we need it very badly."

And so the silent tussle of coping began for both of us, for now what was natural and normal to me, Aunt Betty couldn't seem to grasp. For instance, when she asked me a question I would answer, but many times it was nonverbal, when according to my old culture it was appropriate to do so by using my chin or at other times my lower lip. In cases such as these, after a few minutes wait, when I was busy with something else, she would ask me why I hadn't answered her. For a long time I couldn't figure out why she would ask me a question when her back was to me, or why she wouldn't look at me for her answer. I had been taught to use my eyes, ears, and nose before I ever used my mouth, but these people, kind though they were, used their mouths all of the time. I had also been taught to listen, watch, and wait for the answer to a question I might have to reveal itself, but these people said "Why" all of the time about anything and everything. Another confusing thing for me was also due to my cultural upbringing. When someone asked me a question, I was supposed to figure out what the answer was that the questioner wished to hear, and that would become my answer. Here, everyone asked so many questions that I had no time to figure out what the answers were that they wished to hear. It was very frustrating not knowing how to respond correctly.

The day that I arrived I noticed that the Thompson family had a yellow and green budgerigar (a parakeet native to Australia) in their home. The first time I saw it, I couldn't believe my eyes, for why would anyone keep a bird in their home and in a cage? Did they know that it would not get any bigger? Were they trying to fatten it up? It was all by itself. Had they had others and eaten them? I asked no questions as I waited and watched with much curiosity and inward speculation concerning the fate of the bird.

Aunt Betty was (and is) a very striking looking lady with an abundance of deep, auburn-colored hair, which she kept in beautiful order. She seemed to have only two fears: one in regards to mice in the house, and the other of their bird getting out of the cage and getting into her hair.

One day the Thompson boys decided to try and see if I would scare like their Mum, who always went into her room and shut the door until they had promised that the bird was once again secure in its cage. As they reached in to get the bird out of its cage, with the intent of making it fly at me, I ruthlessly informed them that if I caught it, I got to cook and eat it as I had many others like it. Although they were not really sure I was serious, they were very quick to catch the bird and return it to its cage. In future they kept a wary eye on me whenever I came near their bird's cage. For a long time the purpose of the bird remained a mystery to me, and then one day I learned about the custom of having a pet, and letting it live in the house.

I was soon accepted or at least tolerated by the Thompson boys, since I did not scare easily with bugs or creepy crawlers.

Now wee Kathy fascinated me for she was a beautiful little copy of her Mum, and so very lady-like. Small I was, lady-like I was not, for I had often been called a tomboy.

There was a day early on in my life with them, in which we had been indoors and rather boisterous all afternoon due to another cold winter snow storm. Aunt Betty was almost at the end of her patience with us. She was talking, and talking, and the four of us children were not paying much attention, until she said something that I couldn't figure out, and I questioned her – "what was traffic?" This was probably one of the first questions I ever asked. I thought we had been told to do something and I wanted to be obedient, but did not know what I was supposed to do. She explained that the road right in front of the house with cars driving back and forth was traffic. What she had said was "you are all making so much noise, why don't you all just go out and play in the traffic." I had gotten up, walked to the door, put my hand on the knob to open it, when I heard this urgent voice saying, "Marilyn, where are you going?" I replied with my hand still on the knob, "you said, go play in traffic." I then dimly remembered hearing the children laugh when she had said it. I now saw from the look on her face that something was wrong, but what? How very frustrated and stupid I felt, for even when I tried to do things right and obey, it was wrong. Why did they sometimes say what they didn't mean at all?

The last part of verse two in Psalms 122 in the Living Bible describes perfectly the watchful attitude by which I lived. It reads like this – "or a slave girl watches her mistress for the slightest signal." Now I wasn't a slave girl, but as a foster child I was constantly alert for subtle hints given (many times unconsciously) by the family. I had to learn quickly how they expected me to react in each new situation. Everything had to be learned, starting with where, when, and how I was to sit at the table, to whatever unspoken rules this family had that I might violate unintentionally.

Grandma Thompson lived nearby, and sometimes when she came for a special get-together or a meal, she would make and bring cookies. These biscuits were like nothing I had ever tasted and just melted in my mouth, like the woven sugar spun on leaves by ants back home, but better. I soon learned that they were called shortbread cookies. Whenever "Grandma" came with her "cookies," I was always horribly tempted to take a couple of extra to hoard and eat in private a little at a time, but I managed to resist just in case here it would be considered stealing. It sure was hard to be good.

I had grown up eating wild, naturally-grown, mild, and bland food with no spices. I was not used to anything with a strong smell or taste; whereas, they liked turnips (turn-up-your-nose I called them), rutabaga, and onions. Just like in my real home, here too, if we didn't like a food, we only had to have just a tiny bit of it, and we were allowed to dish up our own plates. I was really thankful that they put bread on the table at meal times, for it often helped me get food down without tasting it.

Recess & Reading

With each letter I received I hoped to hear what was really going on with my friends, brother, and parents, but Mum rarely ever mentioned anything specific at all. Mum later said that she did not want to worry me by writing about the camp fights as to who was injured or even their illnesses. Her reasoning was that by the time I got the letter, which often was at least a month or even two after it had been written, everything was long past and no longer relevant. Since they avoided telling me much at all about what was taking place at Cundeelee, I began to think that they were purposely cutting me out of their lives. It wasn't long before I decided that I could play that game too. I would survive and not let anyone get close to me ever again, and since they didn't seem to care about me, so I wouldn't care about them either. Although I loved them, I tried not to think about my folks very often because of the overwhelming feelings of loss, betrayal, and confusion I felt over being abandoned by them to an unknown family.

I continued to get intermittent letters from Mum always telling me to be a good girl and asking about school, as to what subjects I was enjoying, and what class I liked the best. Without fail every letter she received from me (verified by Mum) had recess as my one and only favorite "subject," and that I hated school. Most of my classmates, as well as their brothers and sisters, had been going to this school for what seemed like forever to me. They not only knew all about farming, but also all about each other; whereas, I knew nothing about living on a farm, let alone in a town or city. Therefore I was "fair game" and oh so gullible.

The teachers were caring individuals, concerned that we pay attention and learn; however, there was no creativity allowed – just book learning. I had so many gaps it was hard to build when I didn't know the fundamentals, whether it had to do with spelling or math. I had moved most of my grades up from F to D and a lot later up to all C's. A's were from 90 – 100 (A+ being 100), B's were from 80 – 89, and C's were from 70 – 79. The only A's that I received were when we were allowed to recite orally our memory work and not write it.

Our English teacher, a Miss Duke, worked so very hard tapping the board with her ruler, while going over and over words being nouns, adjectives, prepositions etc., until I could quote her sayings, but couldn't grasp the idea. What new twist was this English language taking? Was she trying to tell me that there was a hidden meaning to these words? It certainly wasn't a tonal thing. "My language" was not a descriptive one, nor were the sentences constructed in the same order. For instance if I were to say to someone – "Do you see that old man over there?" What I would actually say and do would be as follows. If I did not have the full attention of the person I planned to talk to I would say "Wati Tjilpi" (man old) and then use either my chin or lower lip to point him out. If they were looking at me I would first indicate by one of the above gestures about whom I was talking. My language was so simple, for it was mainly the tone of voice that indicated whether I was making a statement or asking a question. Just the facts or words needed to convey meaning were used, but here the teacher wanted to know about hidden meanings to every word. She seemed to be such a stern person, and I heard people say that she was a very tough lady. She drilled and drilled us, wanting perfection, but in spite of her tough demeanor she had kind eyes, and a small twitch of a smile when she was pleased with something or someone.

In time I had a favorite subject besides recess, all thanks to my eighth-grade teacher, Miss Armstong. Looking back I can see there were other students, mainly from the nearby farms, who were also having trouble with their school lessons. Anytime there were crops to plant or harvest, the boys especially, had to stay at home and work until the farm needs were met. Then they returned to school. Miss Armstrong was very quick to realize that she needed to get us interested in reading not just our school lessons, but books. She was looking ahead for us when being able to read would be a very important skill in our lives.

One day when we came in from lunch, she told us to put our heads down on the top of our desks and watch the picture unfold in our mind of what was going on as she read. Slowly, but with great emphasis she proceeded to read, and we to listen, to a story about a horse. About a half-an-hour later she stopped at a crucial spot and put the book away. Miss Armstrong did this every school day right after lunch, reading through well-known (but not to us) stories about animals, people who did noble acts, and of far away places. Then one day she didn't finish the book, but rather just left us hanging, and started another, and then another. Later she just read to the middle of an exciting spot. Her ploy worked, for soon we were going to the library to find out the endings to the stories. I am so thankful for caring people and teachers who entered my life when I desperately needed them. At the time I did not realize it, but my life was enriched and blessed for all time because of them. They not only taught me the scriptures and values that would stick with me for the rest of my life, but also the pleasure and understanding that comes with the ability to read and "see" as I read.

Then came the day when in a letter to my folks I put recess as number one, and added reading as number two, but still included my usual about hating everything else about school, and to please come and get me.

Birthday & Boys

The Thompson home in which I was living was the last one in a row of homes and situated on a very busy corner. In front of the house was a sidewalk, then a road, and on the other side of the road stood a low building called the print shop. Behind the print shop were the men's (Bible College) dorms, which were called J and K. I believe that all of the dorms, whether for males or females, were four stories high. To our left was a row of homes, and behind us was H or the high school boys' dorm. Next to the right side of the house was a cement sidewalk with a steam tunnel running underneath it, then a small parking lot, and a huge building called "The Tabernacle" where we attended church services.

Regardless of whether I went into the back yard to play, or out the front door, I always felt as if male eyes were staring down at me. Since the dorms were built up so high I felt very vulnerable with no place to hide. Men walked back and forth to classes past our house from early morning to late at night and at all hours in between. Some of the men, trying to be friendly, would say "hi" or try to chat. Each time I would try to quickly move out of their view by going behind one of the kids, the fence, or back into the house.

I was still coping with terrifying nightmares of someone trying to get me, and would awaken in a cold sweat and my heart hammering night after night. I was living with sensory overload trying to memorize all of the male faces going by, and categorizing them in my mind by their actions and body language. I placed each in one of three categories, which were good or nice, arrogant or be wary of, and then the last were where my gut feeling said to stay far away from them at all times.

At the Thompson home we didn't have company very often, and especially not men from the college. One particular night we had two men come for supper who both had the same first name. Now I had seen these two from time to time, walking by the house on their way to class, and while one was always pleasant to everyone, the other one was in my "arrogant and be wary of" category.

This particular evening was no different in that I didn't say anything and just nodded to them when I was introduced. It was then that I received a frightening shock, for I found out that they had been invited mainly to see me. Fear was all that was needed to lock my jaw shut and determine not to say anything to them, but soon the reason turned into hurt and anger as well. We sat at the table and while everyone was eating and talking, the "arrogant" fellow leaned across the table towards me and grinned. I took it as a sort of jeer, and then he said to me, "We just came from Australia, I mean Cundeelee where we have been living for several months with your folks." He looked like he was just taunting me with the information and wanted me to beg him to tell me all, which of course I stubbornly would not lower myself to do. The first thing I thought was that he was "putting me on," but looking at his gloating face I knew he was telling the truth. He said some words in Wangatha, which though poorly pronounced confirmed the truth of his statement. I would not stoop to his level to either correct his pronunciation, or acknowledge that I recognized what he had said in any way. I sat very still staring at him unblinking for a few seconds before putting my head back down, and then went back to eating my food as if I could neither see nor hear him. As he talked he gloated over the things they had seen and done while they were at Cundeelee. I could not understand how my parents could have them at Cundeelee, and not me. In my mind, I could see all of my friends and the things he was talking about, and here I was stuck in this cold country far from family. It just didn't seem fair. I had tried to be so very good for so long now. It was almost too much to bear - the overwhelming feeling of being homesick, lonely, and yes, very jealous of these two men. I tried to listen as the other fellow, quietly answered questions, and maybe would have talked to him, but the fellow across from me was not done yet in trying to destroy my fragile shell. When supper was over he pulled something out of his pocket, and handed it to me saying that my Mum, known as Aunty Ethel to him and the people of Cundeelee, had asked them to bring me my birthday present. (It was the only one I can ever remember receiving from them during those years, due in part to customs and part to lack of money.) I wondered how Mum could have given this fellow anything to give to me, for the other fellow was much nicer. Watching both of them I reasoned that Mum had probably given it to the nice one, but the other fellow had coerced him into letting him give it to me, for their natures seemed to bear this out. By now everyone was saying, "Open it, lets see what it is," and all the while I wanted to just hold, and savor it. I wanted to open it in private later. Once again obeying, I opened it so all could see the lovely rhinestone broach of a Kangaroo sitting in a Boomerang. Underneath the broach was a note in Mum's hand writing, which said "Happy Birthday, Marilyn, Love Dad & Mum."

I never spoke the entire time that they were there. I knew that if I did I would either cry and shame myself, or say something in Wangatha, which I shouldn't, and they just might know a bad word if they heard it. I wanted to scream, yell, wail in frustration and anger, but instead stayed seemingly calm and oh so silent. When they went to leave I could tell by their body language, from the lifting of their shoulders, and the tone of their voices (especially the one) that in spite of enjoying a home-cooked meal they were glad to have completed their duty call. Aunt Betty tried to get me to say thank you to them, but I just couldn't; however, when she said thank you, I nodded my head in agreement. It was the best I could do. I never got another chance to talk to or thank the nice fellow, and have often regretted not doing so at the time.

That night, long after everyone was in bed and sound asleep, I pulled my pillow over my head and cried and cried. I fell asleep crying, only to awaken in terror in the middle of the night due to having another violent nightmare. I was so very tired of having bad dreams that I decided to do the only thing I could think of that could possibly help me, and that was to pray. I had prayed before with the normal type of, "now I lay me," and "please no dreams," but it was time to get really serious. I believed in prayer, but I wasn't so sure that God was listening to me, for so far my prayers about going back to Australia had not been answered in the way I wanted. Although it was cold, since it was the middle of a winter night and we kids had rooms in the attic, I crawled out of bed. Kneeling beside my bed I asked Jesus to please, please stop these awful horrible bad dreams and not let them come back, for I was exhausted, tired and scared.

I got back into bed totally wiped out by the events of the day and promptly fell back asleep. Once again a miracle happened, for it was well over a year before I had a dream that I could even remember, let alone wake from in terror.

Machines & Music

I was very curious about the contents of the building that sat right across the road from the Thompson home. The building labeled "Print Shop." Sometimes I would hear weird sounding noises emanating from there, and I just couldn't figure out what or who would make those kinds of sounds. The day came when I was allowed to go into this building with an adult, and could check out for myself what went on in there. There were metal things going up and down as well as some going side to side. There were other things going around that reminded me of my dad's razor strap, only they were much larger, and traveled in circles around round metal rods. There were stacks of paper on shelves and in front of machines in varying shape, sizes and colors. Instead of being exciting it was rather dismal, dirty, noisy, and had a peculiar odor. As I watched, a person pushed a stack of about ten folded papers onto a machine, which gave a great whack, and suddenly it was held together with little metal things called staples. Since I was watching this machine intently, and the noise level was quite high, it took me a second or two before I realized that I was being spoken to, and asked if I would like to try it. He went over the whole procedure from picking up and tapping the papers to sliding the papers just so onto the machine, and concluded with where to place the booklet after the papers had been stapled. I was watched while I did several leaflets and then I was on my own. I did very well until I got a little tired, let my mind wander, and goofed up nearly stapling my fingers. Next thing I knew I was working part time in the Print Shop, and no longer had to worry about the scary noises that came out of that building. From this job I learned that not only did I enjoy working with my hands, but also that I could do something right, and maybe just a little of me wasn't stupid after all. It was at this point in time that I realized I didn't need to understand every word of direction spoken to me. As long as I could see it done, I could copy the action precisely.

Other than the songs and choruses that Dad and Mum had taught us at Cundeelee, the only "music" with which I was familiar was a type of chant. Here I was hearing choirs, soloists, and musicians playing instruments, which were so beautiful I just wanted to sit, listen, and lose myself from my present surroundings. I learned to enjoy a variety of music, through the radio, their record player, and the great college choir at the school. I can remember two specific records that we played so often we almost wore them and Aunt Betty's patience out. One record comprised of a song written by a missionary lady while she was dying of cancer. She had taken the words of some of the verses from Psalms 51, and had made it into a song. In my mind's eye I can still see her and her husband down front in the tabernacle teaching us this song as she played her guitar. It had a very singable tune, and at times I can still hear the words and the music running through my head, but others who heard this same song cannot remember it at all. As I remember, the title was: -

"A Contrite Heart" and the words went something like this -
A contrite heart I offer thee dear Savior,
Oh pardon Lord, this soul that went astray,
Make me to know once more thy joy and gladness,
Oh purify my heart, without, within.
I humbly now acknowledge my transgressions,
Against thee, Holy Father, have I sinned,
Restore to me, once more thy joy and gladness,
Oh purify my heart, without, within.

I reckon that the boys' and my all time favorite record to play when we were especially uptight, angry, plain out-of-sorts, or even sometimes just for fun, was the 1812 Overture by Tchaikovsky. We especially liked to turn the volume way up when the drums and cymbals were at their loudest and just savor the satisfying noise. This was before head sets and earphones, and what one heard everyone in the house heard as well. Aunt Betty was really quite tolerant, but enough is sometimes shorter for adults than for pesky children pushing their limits.

I loved to listen to the choir practicing in the tabernacle next door. The pianist for the choir was a Miss Kathleen Dearing, the sister of the Principal, Ruth Dearing, of the grade school and high school. Miss Kathleen had graduated at the top of her class at the Toronto Conservatory of Music. Instead of going on to make a name for herself publicly, she had instead come to this small school and dedicated herself to teach and play for God's glory. She was truly an awesome pianist. Her fingers just dancing across the keys so fast and lightly, that it seemed as if she never touched them, but that they just sang for her. I so loved to watch, as much as to hear her play, that I decided that I would like to learn how to play the piano for myself.

Now the only previous experience that I had of anyone learning how to play a musical instrument had been an Aboriginal boy named Ron. After hearing a song only one time I had seen him play the song on whatever musical instrument there was at hand. I had seen him play a mouth organ, pump organ, and even a guitar, note for note, after he had heard a song played one time. I had never been in a school that had a school choir or band, and here the music appreciation class consisted of listening to records that were played in class by the teacher. Once in a great while we had a live pianist come to the school and play for us. I don't remember hearing anyone other than the Thompson boys playing scales and wondered why they would play anything so meaningless. I could hum a tune, and could also pick up immediately on a missed or incorrect note so I thought, quite erroneously, that I would be able to play immediately just like I had seen Ron do back home. Oh, those awful scales, and holding my hands just so - let alone trying to figure out what all of those little squiggles meant. They were like another foreign language, and I was having a hard enough time with English. Needless to say my attempt to learn to play the piano lasted less than six months and ended in eroding the last of my self-confidence and my ability to learn new things. I was so disappointed in myself for not being able to figure out and follow the "tracks" on the paper. It reinforced my perception that anything I did in this foreign country so far from home was doomed for failure. From now on I would just enjoy listening and forget any idea I might have had about learning to play a musical instrument. For the first time in my life I realized that my tenacity to hang in there had to take a back seat to my emotional survival. I don't know who was more relieved when I quit piano lessons – my piano teacher, the Thompson family, or me.

Rules & Roommates

1959 rolled in starting another year that would be full of changes, and new challenges.

By February, Dale, who had endured two years of teasing and harassment, from short sheets and knives pulled on him, to a hose soaking his bed late at night, decided that he had stayed in Canada long enough. He returned to the Seattle area with the intent of getting to know his grandparents and nearby relatives. On his arrival he was shocked, angry, and saddened to learn that our Grandpa Stewart had died just weeks before his return. Dale would miss the smell of leather, the gently pounding hammer, and getting to know his grandpa better. Grandpa Stewart had been a shoemaker, quiet man, and a good listener. After Dale had been in Seattle for a while he joined the service. For over a year I had no idea as to his whereabouts or even how he could be located. It was as if he too had disappeared for good and I felt even more insecure in this strange world. My immediate family members were now spread in three different countries.

The Bible School students got out of school in April, and resumed again in October. Getting out this early allowed them to find good summer jobs in their hometowns, or towns and farms near the school that needed workers. Over the years students attending this school had built a great reputation in the area for being honest and hard working people. The tourist town of Banff employed a lot of women from the school during the summer. They worked as receptionist, cooks, cleaned cabins, did laundry and office work.

The summer of the previous year, Darlene had stayed on campus to work at and for the school and planned to do it again the summer of 1959. After a girl suddenly quit working at a motel in Banff, Darlene was called and asked if she would like to take her place. Since it was a lot more money, which Darlene needed badly in order to pay her college expenses, she immediately said "yes."

Even though I had rarely seen my brother and sister, I had felt relatively secure just knowing they were not too far away on this large campus. Now I felt that I really was on my own, for both of them had disappeared in less than three months. Where they were or how far they had gone I didn't know. It was sort of like the Aborigines going "Walk-About" – where they went or how long they'd be gone we never knew until they suddenly turned up again. It could be months or it could even be a couple of years – so too now, I would wait for my brother and sister to return. I sure hoped everyone hadn't abandoned me here for good.

In the fall of that year Mrs. Thompson and I felt that it was time for me to go and live in the high school girls' dorm. I was now going into ninth grade, and the Thompson family was going to increase by one more in the coming year. I thought that they needed the space, and time together without me being around. Besides as nice as they were to me, I really was an outsider. I often ached inside with longing to be with my real family, and still could not figure out why they had not taken me back with them to Australia. I had two major reasons that I did not voice, but were the prime reasons I wished to leave the comfort of their home. My most important reason was to get out from under the constantly watching male eyes from the nearby men's dorms. It would be such a huge relief to get out of their sight, and whistles, and the constant fear I had of one of them attacking me. The other reason was to get to see my sister Darlene a little more often, even if it was only a reassuring glimpse of her as she walked by my dorm on her way to and from classes. "The powers that be" had rarely approved Darlene coming to visit me when I lived at the Thompson home, for it was located between the High School Boys' dorm, and the College men's dorm. This territory was out of bounds to unmarried female students.

It didn't take much time or effort on my part to be ready to move out of the Thompson home, since all I possessed was a small suitcase of clothes, a Bible, and the doll I had gotten in Kalgoorlie when I was ill. I wanted to give them something to show how thankful I was to them for the care they had given to me, so I gave little Kathy my prized doll. I remember Aunt Betty saying "Marilyn, are you sure that you want to give your doll to her?" and I said "yes." Their decision to care for me had cost them, so in my mind it was right that in return I leave something of value to me. The only thing that I had to give was my doll, which I knew Kathy liked very much.

The first week of dorm life was a bit daunting, for everything revolved around ringing bells, buzzers, school, and work. Six in the morning was the time to rise and shine, according to the first bell. At twenty-five after there was a five-minute warning buzzer with the next bell at six-thirty. This one meant you had better be getting dressed, because the monitor was coming around to make sure. Each room had a basin and a pitcher, but the bathrooms and showers were located at the end of the hall on each floor. Five til seven and then at seven the buzzer, then the bell, signaled a quiet half hour for devotions, though some did try to finish their school work, and were sorry indeed if they were caught. Bells, five-minute warning buzzers, and bells again were heard at intervals throughout the entire day. Before going to breakfast we had to line up in the hall with our coats on, to have our skirt or dress checked for length from the floor. If cleared by the monitor we had to go straight to the dining room, and not allowed to return to our room in case we changed clothes. In the dining room we had to remove and hang up our coat, find our assigned seat and be seated, when the bell rang at eight. If we were late it was demerit time, which meant extra gratis work. In the High School Girls' dorm the last bell of the day rang at nine-thirty, which signaled lights out. During the next hour or two the monitor would check several times for any light noise or activity taking place, in any of the rooms.

Since I had been late registering for a dorm room, the first room assigned to me was a converted closet. The bed just barely fit and I had no table, but I was finally alone and the relief was unbelievable. I, who had been so used to roaming the Outback by myself, had conformed to everyone for so long, that it was heavenly to be totally by myself. I could talk quietly to myself in my own language without someone over hearing, and I didn't have to worry every second about not doing something right.

All too soon there were a couple of rooms available due to several students departing. A reshuffle, a move on my part and I became a roommate. The policy was that everyone had to have a roommate. It was considered to be part of the discipline to learn how to get along with another person in very close quarters, as well as a way to encourage us to make new friends.

During the next two years I had several roommates, all from other countries. My first roommate was from Africa, where her parents were missionaries. The sound of her voice made me homesick, for she spoke with a British accent. She not only spoke excellent English (for she had gone to a boarding school in Africa); she also spoke a little Swahili. She seemed to know exactly what she wanted, and how she was going to achieve it, while I silently wondered how she could be so sure of getting what she desired. Any time either of us became especially frustrated, whether it was with the other person, or our own peculiar circumstances, we would rattle off words in another language. It was in this way that we managed to let off some steam without feelings being hurt. We had found not only a great safety valve, but also a way to avoid confrontations. After several months had passed, she somehow got her wish and was able to return to Africa and her family. I never figured out how she was able to accomplish such a feat and so quickly.

My next roommate was the youngest of five being left at the boarding school. There were seven kids in her family, but the two younger children were returning to South America with their parents. The rule in the High School dorm was that no one could room with relatives, and that everyone had to room with someone they didn't know. Now my new roommate did not like this rule at all, and cried all of the time, and I mean all. I knew she was very homesick, but she at least had a sister in the same dorm, another in the dorm next to us, as well as two brothers on campus, and they all got together every Sunday. Day after day she'd cry, and then she started crying selectively when someone who could help her "cause" was in her vicinity. We had weeks and weeks of commotion as her sisters and the dorm counselors came and went from our room trying to counsel and console her. They were also busy telling me that she should not have to help clean our room, and that I should pamper her more and give in to her every whim. I was instructed to do everything I could to make her want to room with me and not her sister. Then the sisters' started giving me dirty looks whenever they saw me. This continued even after she got what she wanted, which was to room with her sister. I was really at a loss to figure out what I could have done differently. She wanted to room with her sister, and had figured out a way to accomplish it. In the meantime she'd made my life extremely uncomfortable due to her and her sisters antics and the rebukes I received from the dorm counselors. I later realized that the sister was older and happy to be rooming with a girl her age, and now was stuck instead with her younger, very spoiled sister. I had never seen anyone throw such tantrums and get rewarded for it – this was indeed a strange New World. For a time I was once again without a roommate. I was thankful for the sudden peace and time to recover emotionally from what I considered had been unwarranted attacks on me.

I seemed to please no one, regardless of how hard I thought I was trying. In school, certain teachers using long rulers, would hit my desk and a few times my knuckles, while saying, "Marilyn you are not trying hard enough." These were usually teachers who had taught my sister and brother before me. I often stayed after class for help, but usually didn't know or understand what they were talking about, so it did little good, though it made the teachers happy.

One day our teacher said that a new student would be joining our class shortly - a girl from Brazil. Knowing how hard it had been, and still was, for me to understand things, I wanted her to feel welcome from the very first day. I helped her settle into her room, showed her where things were and whenever I saw her I asked her how she was doing etc. – just tried to be a friend. I didn't want her to experience the same cold shoulder type of treatment from the students that I had on arriving. I was to find out that she did not need my help or concern for she was a real "smart cookie." She spoke to the teachers using a thick accent and very broken English about how hard it was for her to keep up. They not only allowed her more time to finish assignments, but also in some cases cut down her required homework and tests. It was unbelievable! Then one day, walking down the hall in the dorm, I overheard her speaking with another girl. She sounded different for she only had a very slight accent. She caught my look, which must have reflected my puzzlement and surprise for with a slight shrug of her shoulders she calmly said, "use whatever works." It turned out that she had studied English for a couple of years in Brazil, and as a result was much more fluent than I. My disillusionment in people grew for I had considered her to be a new friend, but after this episode she began to seek and hang out only with the "money set" of girls. I was learning that people here were not always what they seemed, which made life far more difficult than in the Outback.

My last roommate came from a wealthy white South African family. They had sent over five young people who were related either as immediate family members or cousins. Although my new roommate was a very open and friendly individual she had a lot of money, clothes, and definite ideas in regard to status. She was tall, (5'7" to an almost 5'3" person is tall) as well as being blond, beautiful, and the owner of a big smile. We got along fine as roommates, but we sadly never bonded as really good friends. I always felt that it was partly due to my quiet nature, and the differences in our backgrounds and status, or lack of it. She was used to having servants, whereas I was still very naïve, and just learning that to some people all men were not considered their equal.

Each morning we dutifully lined up in the hall to have our hems checked in relationship to the floor. While my hems had to be at least two inches below my knees, my roommate, who was four inches taller than I, only had to have hers just below her kneecap. One day she loaned me a pretty pink mohair jacket and skirt to wear since it was uncomfortably tight on her. The skirt just barely covered her knees and had been certified as okay for her to wear. That morning I confidently walked up to the monitor knowing that this time all would be fine, but no, it was too short! I had to go and change clothes. Neither my roommate nor I ever figured out how the inches from the floor had been calculated. Many a morning we stood in line waiting while a new monitor checked the chart to see what was wrong, because everyone's hem was supposed to be well below the knee. It remained an unsolved riddle till the day I departed, but we wondered if it had something to do with our age for she was a year younger.

She not only had relatives that she spent a lot of time with in other parts of the dorm, she also had lots of money to spend every other Saturday afternoon we "ladies" were permitted to walk to town. One Saturday the men could walk to town and the next Saturday the women could walk in that direction. I had never been allowed to just go to a refrigerator and take out anything I wanted to eat or drink. For years we didn't have one; then when we did, it was hands off unless I was setting a table, and the same held true when living in foster homes. There were no refrigerators, cool chests or hot plates allowed at any time anywhere in the dorm. Not having been accustomed to shopping for clothes or going to town and having cookies, pop, and candy regularly, I never missed it, but my poor roommate suffered. Being allowed to go to town and shop only twice in a month was pure agony for her. She did eventually learn to stock up and ration her supplies, but she missed being daily in and out of "shops," as had been her habit.

After we'd been roommates for a couple of months, one of her cousins said to her in my presence, that she treated me just like one of her servants back home, to which she replied "Why not, she doesn't mind." I was beginning to mind very much.

Each one of my roommates knew what they wanted and figured out a way to make it happen. Why couldn't I get what I wanted? To my way of thinking, I wanted only a very small thing. Just one desire was all - just to get back to being "A Child of the Outback in Australia." In the two and a half years I lived in the dorm I saw a great deal of underhanded dealings; some just puzzled me but others shocked me. My culture frowned on such behavior and so I waited, never thinking of doing something myself other than try to be good and patient. I had not learned how to think or act for myself for someone was always telling me what to do and when to do it.

At the time I did not realize, because I was silently working so hard to not be seen as different, I was doing too good a job at copying. People were accepting me at face value, never understanding I was starting almost everything with no foundation on which to build.

Except for my white skin, which blended in with almost everyone on campus, I was in reality a "minority" in my culture, language and upbringing.

Most days my life seemed joyless and very scary.

Peeling & Praises

As dorm students we were each required to put in one-and-a-half hours of work per day. In this way tuition costs were kept lower than most schools, and the work that needed doing each day was accomplished. We had very little free time to get into trouble, and we learned how to work hard at whatever job we were assigned. I soon learned the value of doing every job thoroughly the first time for the consequence of sloppy work was additional work. This daily work was referred to as gratis, and changed every quarter as to the type of work we performed. Gratis ranged from working in the laundry, sorting and washing clothes, to office work. The older and more skilled students got jobs grading papers, sorting mail, working in the infirmary, and office work. I was young and unskilled, so in my years there I swept floors, cleaned and set tables, and worked over and over again in the peeling room. Every afternoon after school I'd be late for my mandatory "gratis" unless I ran from school to the dorm, dropped my books, made the quickest of bathroom stops, and again ran to the peeling room. The next one-and-a-half hours I, along with others, cleaned, peeled, and cut up enough vegetables to feed between 800 and 1000 people the following day. We worked three hours on Saturday mornings in order to have Sundays off.

In the peeling room were three long stainless steel tables with six-inch high sides, which kept the vegetables from falling on the floor. Once the vegetables were poured onto the tables, we were assigned a spot to stand. The cement floor was so cold some days that it seemed to almost freeze our feet in place. We peeled and cut up onions, carrots, potatoes, beets, rutabagas, etc. as fast as we could. If we were doing a good job, after a while we were allowed to talk quietly to the person next to us. I did say this was only "women's" work, didn't I? Once in a great while if a person really was not feeling well, they were allowed to sit on a high stool providing their work did not slow down. If our monitor felt in a good mood, but didn't want us to talk, she would start us singing. It was during one of these times of singing that I learned not everyone could stay on the right notes or "carry a tune." One day, a girl I was just getting to know was allowed to stand next to me while we worked. I had noticed that when she talked, whether excited or not, she talked in a flat straight-line type of voice with no variation at all except in volume. This particular day was one of our relatively "light" days, so we were allowed to sing. A song was picked and the starting note was hummed and then just as I started to sing a funny thing happened. I heard a hearty loud voice right next to me "singing," but the tune never once varied either up or down. At first I tried to block it out and sing, but soon I could no longer keep on the right note myself. I silently wondered if she knew that she wasn't singing the same tune as the others. I had given up singing altogether when I heard a whisper near my ear saying that she knew she could not sing a note, but once-in-a-while she just had to let go and "make a joyful noise." I was very surprised, almost shocked even, to realize that I could do something that my new, out-going confident friend could not. She later confided to me that when she got to Heaven her request would be for a beautiful singing voice for she planned to do a lot of singing to make up for her lack of ability while on earth. I thought to myself, that in heaven I not only wanted a beautiful voice, but also to be able to play a musical instrument skillfully.

Each Sunday morning after we had a big breakfast we were given two slices of bread and "fixings" to make a sandwich, which would become our lunch. Church was held in the tabernacle and sometimes the service lasted for two hours. The main speaker was usually the President of the School. I watched almost mesmerized, as he rarely stood still for an instant, but walked, crouched, pointed and shouted. As the months passed I began to realize that he was preaching about the same God as my Dad, but he used big words and pounded the pulpit with his fist and hollered so loudly I was afraid. The music was awesome, whether it was a solo, hymns the audience sang, or the musicians skillful playing, but to me the best part of the service each week was listening to the choir. Oh, my, but they sounded heavenly. After our sandwich lunch, which we consumed in our dorm room, we could lay down for a nap, go visit a friend in the dorm, or go for a walk, but sometime that afternoon we had to write a letter to a parent or guardian. Before we were allowed to sit down and eat supper that evening we had to hand to the monitor a stamped and addressed letter. Sometimes we had to leave the envelope unsealed and it was checked to see if there was a letter or just blank pages inside. No letter, no meal.

With so much negativity in my life, hearing such unbelievably beautiful music on Sundays was a special treat and I could listen to it "singing in my head" for days afterwards. The music was like a healing touch of blessing to my dry soul.

Farms & Felines

During these four long years, two happy, relaxing events took place, which were filled with much light-hearted fun. The events, which took place a year apart, were engineered by girls at school and occurred during summer holidays. Of course it was Dorothy who first enriched my life by initiating me to life on a farm. I could hardly contain myself when I was invited to spend the summer on their farm. I wanted to sing, dance, run and yet at the same time sit perfectly still and soak in the peaceful stillness of the country. It was glorious to be away from people and noise, to be able to roam and watch the chooks, which were known here as chickens, and to go barefoot while working in the garden. It was pure bliss. We were expected to work, and we did, from feeding the pigs, chickens, and calves to weeding the garden. There were eleven cats in the barn. One had kittens while I was there so we gave them secret coded names in accordance to how we thought their natures in future would match up with some of the boys in our class at school. One I remember we named Archie for a boy in class that bore the initials R.G. and was the heartthrob of most of the girls in class. These kittens provided us with many a lighthearted conversation and giggle, which lightened our spirits. I learned how to milk a cow, and I even managed a time or two to hit a waiting cat in the mouth with a stream of warm fresh milk. I learned how to use a machine called a separator, which separated the cream from the milk. It was also my job to take it apart, wash and scald it until it was sparkling clean and put it back together again.

The big meal of the day was always in the evening when our chores were done, and was usually vegetables and potatoes from the garden, gravy, and meat. I know that Dorothy asked several times if I could come for a visit before her folks finally invited me to come. Her Dad was not too sure about me coming, thinking I might be too high and mighty and look down on them. The first night that I was there her father said, while looking at me, "we only have plain food to eat in this house." That night we had either elk or deer meat, and the next night it was bear, but we never had beef since it was being raised for profit and not for their table. I really enjoyed the wild flavor of the meat since it was the closest thing to kangaroo meat I had tasted in a very long time. There was an older and younger sister at home and no boys, which made it a special, relaxing, happy time with plenty of work and no worries. All too soon my summer holiday was over, but lucky me, the day that I was to return to town it snowed, and snowed. We were snowed in, but eventually I returned to town riding the school bus with Dorothy.

In winter when we donned our ice skates, the boys played hockey and the girls played a similar game using an old broom and a ball the size of a Volleyball. The game was referred to as "Broomball." I had weak ankles, but really enjoyed trying to learn to skate. A couple of times I was invited to go ice skating out at my friend's farm. There was a pond and a creek nearby that froze over and was a challenge, but great fun to try to skate on. All around the edges dried grass poked through the ice, and often the ice had frozen when it was windy making the surface wavy and tough to skate on. I used to like to look down through the ice to see the different layers and what was trapped down there. I was really more interested in the snow and cold beauty around me than in skating.

I had learned as a child in the outback to accept many things, and not to question or judge things quickly, but wait and watch for developments. My background of being in so many types of churches, homes, and situations had also made me open to accepting differences without thinking about them. When I went to the next farm it was a very different experience for me; however, having used my ears well before hand, I realized this family had a farm where they lived in the summer, and a house in town during the winter. Dad had worked for this farmer and knew the family; however, I just knew the daughter from school for we were in the same grade.

I really enjoyed once again being free to roam; however, here we kept our shoes on. We were not expected to do too many chores, and for the most part were treated like pampered young ladies. There were two older sons who helped their father with all of the chores, but one night it was all hands are needed in the field.

It was the proverbial dark and stormy night with rain in the forecast, and hay still lying in the field. The intermittent moon, the truck and bailers' poor headlights were the only lights to pick out what was going on in the field. The father traversed the field in the bailer. This machine cut the hay and spit it out on the ground in regular intervals as a bale. Every bale had a wire wrapped around each end, which not only held it together, but also was useful as handles. The mother drove the truck at an almost standstill crawl along-side the bales. The two of us girls were allowed to share lifting one bale due to the weight and our small size. The older son was on the ground with us hoisting the bales onto the back of the truck. The younger son then stacked it using a predetermined plan. By midnight we were so exhausted that the last couple of bales we tried to lift up, the brothers had to help. We started giggling so we couldn't budge a bale off of the ground. The more disgusted the brothers got, the harder we laughed, until we just plopped down on top of the bale we were trying to lift.

The huge farm truck was stacked well past the top of its railings before a halt was called and the tarp put on to cover most of the hay. Now I learned that we were going to have to crawl up and sit on the top of the bales for our ride home. It had been sprinkling on and off for the last hour with intermittent lightening and thunder rumbling in the distance. Much to the pretended disgust of the young men, we girls were so tired that neither one of us had the strength to get up on the truck without help. The older one got back down and told us to use his back as a step. My friend showed me how by getting onto her brother's back, and then standing up and as he raised up some she was able to grab onto the truck railing and hoist herself up to get a toe under the stacked hay. Once she got on the edge of the truck and stood up, her other brother leaned down, grabbed her wrist and yanked her up onto the top of the hay. When it was my turn I almost panicked when he grabbed my wrist and pulled me up so close to him. I was thankful it was too dark for him to see the fright I felt and the blush that resulted in being so close to him.

The ride home was a real adventure, even at five miles or so an hour, for every time we hit a rut we thought we would all end up on the ground. My feet begin to tingle when I step on the first rung of a ladder, and this was so much higher that I was near panicking. My pride would not allow me to let these young men see how scared I was at being up so high and so close to them.

I eventually found a crevice between the bales to wedge my foot into and then laid on my back watching the sky in an effort to keep my mind off of the ground. It turned into such a lovely night as the clouds parted, the moon shone, no city lights to be seen, and all was still except for the drone of the truck's engine. I could for a few minutes dream that I was back home in my Outback listening to the engine of our old truck.

Varnish & Violence

During the summer of 1959, other than the "farm" holiday, I worked for and at the school. I worked wherever I was assigned, from the print shop to mopping and varnishing floors, mainly in the men's dorms. It had been a real eye opener to see after the no-frills women's dorms, because in the men's dorm there was a lounge and even a Ping-Pong table. When the summer of 1960 came around I was cleared once again to work at the school, but this time I would be living in the dorm with the college women who were remaining. Darlene had once again gotten a job in Banff, but this time it was with the motel across the street from the one she had worked at the summer before. She had told me about seeing bears and how much of a nuisance, and sometimes a threat they were, and about the women she worked with, especially Peaches and Patience. I remember wondering where they had been born and the stories behind their names.

There was one woman who was staying at the school and working there that summer that I just couldn't figure out. She made me feel strangely uneasy. It was not her size or shape, although she was about 5'7" and 200 lbs of pure muscle from working on a farm. When she came near me I was very polite to her; however, since I had lived by obeying my gut feelings, I tried to stay out of her way. One day, just as I was leaving a restroom in the dorm, she walked in and barred my way out. At first I thought of it as pulling rank, and stepped back and to one side, but as she stared at me intently, I became so frightened that I turned to run and hide in one of the stalls. Halfway there she grabbed me, forcing me to my knees saying, "I'll break your back if you don't do what I want you to do." I had no idea what she wanted, but by now she had me wedged between her two legs, and was pushing me backwards over one of them. Someone opening the door to come in saw what was happening to me, and spoke her name in a disgusted tone, adding "let her go." I think I shook with fear all day long, and that night I propped a chair up under the handle of my door. During the summer each of the workers was allowed the luxury of having a room to themselves. I began to fear seeing her, even at a distance, and could hardly work for checking over my shoulder, and could hardly sleep for thinking she would harm me. For a week or two I was able to keep myself near other women and safe, but the evening came when we were all due at a meeting, and I ran late getting my work done. I raced into the dorm as the last of the women were leaving, grabbed my stuff from my room, frantically taking the inside stairs two at a time, only to come face-to-face with this woman as I rounded the corner at the top of the stairs. There was silence for a moment, until she said "got ya," at which time I started to holler, scratch and bite as she drug me down the stairs to my room latching the door behind us. The rooms were so very small that each time I tried to throw my one and only chair out the window she was able to deflect it, as well as keep me away from getting out the window myself. Two hours later we heard sounds of people returning, and with a warning of death if I told anyone that she had been bothering me in any way at all she quickly and quietly left. My room was in shambles from my attempts to escape, my clothes in tatters, my body badly bruised, and my mental well-being extremely precarious.

I could not understand what I had ever done to be assaulted by both a man and a woman both of whom were white, and seemed to be accepted by everyone. What was wrong with me?

To my way of thinking, I could now trust neither men nor women, and yet I must somehow survive and get back "home." I became even more secretive, not wanting anyone to know anything about me and started going to great lengths to avoid being touched. I felt a rush of fear every time a person came too close to me as I tried to figure out where, when, and who might next attack me. I felt beaten and bloodied physically, but my spirit was not bowed, for as far as I was concerned I would continue fighting to survive.

Due to my overwhelmed emotions, by breakfast the next morning I felt like one big quivering mass of unsolidified Jell-O. I dreaded going to breakfast for fear of seeing her, but as she was missing, I was able to eat a small amount of food. My calm lasted only until I was cleaning the tables (my starting job that week) and resetting them for lunch. I was on high alert, and saw her the second she walked through the doors, weaving through the tables, headed in my direction. Keeping my head down while tracking her out of the corner of my eye, I kept moving slowly, yet deliberately, to keep a table between us at all times. I was doing fine until my boss for that week came along and insisted that I come around the table to listen as she talked to me about my assignments for that day. As this woman came up to us, she gave me a sort of knowingly mocking smile, at which my stomach started to rebel. Oh, how I hated for her to know where I was going to be all day long, especially since it was going to be in a rather isolated spot. As my boss was walking away from us this woman made the mistake of reaching for me. As she reached out her hand to touch me, I promptly threw up on her, forcing her, in spite of her dire warnings of what she would do when she caught me, to have to go and change her clothes.

Later that day she found me again; however, this time I was varnishing a dorm room wood floor with the use of a long, flat, old broom. Since I had been on the lookout for her all day and had never turned my back to any doorway, I was quickly able to varnish myself into a corner. She laughed, saying how stupid, to which I icily replied that I would stay there all day if necessary, or jump out the window I was next to, if she dared to come in the room. I added that she'd get varnish on her shoes, which would allow anyone to be able to track her, and know exactly where she had been. I still had the outback mentality of how to find evil doers. After a few more taunts and threats she finally left. It took a while to stop shaking, and even longer to make sure she was really gone. Finally using the flat part of the broom I managed to leave the room with varnish on only one shoe.

That night with the chair firmly in place, I read my Bible as usual, but prayed much more fervently. I told God (as if He didn't already know) that I was exhausted mentally and physically, dreadfully afraid, and just plain scared to bits. Having told God all about it, I was finally able to fall asleep by quoting scripture "promise" verses from the Bible.

Banff & Bears

The very next day a call came from my sister to say that one of the girls had left and there was now an opening at her place of work for me if I wanted it. I had turned sixteen so I could now work away from the school and with her in Banff if I so desired. The owner wanted me there yesterday so to speak. Uncle John Thompson quickly and quietly arranged everything for me. Packing took only minutes to accomplish, and with escape at hand, a very thankful Marilyn boarded the bus alone for the trip to Banff. My prayer for safety had been answered with a job opportunity away from school, but I also had to trust the Lord to keep me safe on the trip to the job. I always seemed to have to do things alone and it was so scary, but I'd not admit that to anyone. I sat up front, close to the driver, and was silent for the whole trip, but my eyes constantly alternated between watching the people around me, and the scenery.

With all the stops the bus made during the 160-mile trip, it was evening before I reached my destination. Upon arrival I was told to immediately report to the office, for the boss was waiting. He proceeded to tell me what would be expected of me as to cleaning the chalets, when I had late night check in duty, and so forth. For the next two days I cleaned motel rooms littered with empty liquor bottles, overflowing ashtrays, and torn up bedding with nary a tip. It was very hard work and I was expected to be fast, efficient and thorough. The third day I was called in and told to report to the lady who ran the laundry. The girl working there had more seniority than I, and had found after three days that she did not like it, plus she wanted the chance to make some tips. At meal times I had heard that the woman who ran the laundry was very hard to please. I was a wee bit anxious that I might not make the grade and instead end up going back to school for the rest of the summer. Darlene encouraged me to just do my best to please the lady, and work hard. As I was walking towards the stairs to the laundry, my pace quickened as a bear came ambling out of the woods about twenty-five feet from me. It was headed in my direction towards several large garbage cans. I had been warned to pound the tin lid on the garbage can if a bear got too close, or between me and where I was headed. This time I was able to race up the stairs and into the laundry without any trouble. It was not very many days later that a bear cub caught Darlene by the ankle. The mother bear was heading for us and the noise from banging the cans seemed futile, but prayer wasn't. Just before the mother reached us the cub let go and ran right into its mother distracting her long enough for us to escape down some nearby stairs.

I entered the laundry rather quickly and neither of us, at first glance, was impressed with what we saw. In her eyes I was much too small, and to me she looked as if she'd never been kind to anyone or anything in her life. My bush training, to use my eyes and ears, before ever using my mouth, once again stood me in good stead. I watched intently everything she did, and copied her without speaking. She rarely ever spoke to me, and when she did it was only to explain something she thought I should know. At the end of the day all she said when I went to leave was, "at least you aren't a chatterbox. I'll see you tomorrow." I was relieved that I still had a job. I liked this job a lot better since there were only two of us working in a huge room. I no longer had to worry about someone surprising (as the owner's son had) and cornering me in one of the rooms I was cleaning. My new assignment was a great boon to my stressed-out system, and I made sure I thanked God for answering my prayer. That night at mealtime, I was asked how the day went and replied "fine," which didn't satisfy the woman who had traded jobs. She continued through supper telling stories of how the "laundry" lady had hollered at her each day all day long and how awful it was to work for her. I suddenly realized the problem had been too much talking, and had nothing to do with the work itself – oh, the relief I felt. I could do this job.

We had a cook at the motel from Hungary. She cooked only for the workers, and every meal, be it breakfast, lunch or dinner, the food was smothered with either raw or cooked onions. By the end of the summer we were begging her to leave at least one meal free of onion as our stomachs felt raw, but she just couldn't cook that way. Therefore, on our day off we usually hiked into town to get something to eat to soothe our so-sore stomachs. We were about two miles up a steep hill from the town of Banff, only got one day off a week, and usually were too tired to walk too far. As workers in the Banff area, we were given free passes to Lake Louise, to the chair lift, and other attractions, but the problem for us was one of our location and transportation, or the lack of it. None of us had access to a car, and there was no such thing as a bus route, so we had to depend on making wise choices in regards to the "rides" we chose when we thumbed a ride. Darlene and I were eventually able to get the same day off, and have an exciting, exhausting, day of sightseeing. We rode the chair lift, went to Lake Louise, had a meal, and were even able to hitch a ride back to the motel at the end of that wonderful memorable day.

One day Darlene and I were called to the office, handed a cablegram and told we could take an extra break. Knowing it had to be bad news we hurried over to a shady spot under a nearby tree and sat down. Darlene opened the cable and read "Mom being taken to hospital. Pray." We knew it was really serious, because this was the only cable we had received from our folks in the three years that they had been gone. I remember thinking that the words on the piece of paper had come so far and told us so little. In spite of my lack of understanding regarding my circumstances, I loved my parents very much. I knew that their work amongst the Aborigines was important and honoring to God. It was several days before the next cable arrived with the good news that Mum was out of danger and would recover.

With my first pay check I put some money aside for a red coat with a white hood that unzipped in the center to lay flat, and the rest went towards my next year's school fees. At the end of the summer I was the very proud owner of two new items that I had bought with my very own hard-earned money. The red coat had been my first buy, and a suitcase that had sliding hinges that allowed it to expand to contain all of my earthly belongings was the other.

In Banff there was a school of fine arts to which students came for the summer to hone their craft. At the mid-point and again at the end of the season they would put on several plays. We were able to go to La Traviata, and A-Mid-Summers-Night-Dream. While I had not the slightest idea of what was going on, it was away from work. I found it interesting to watch the play, the peoples' varying reactions, all the different kinds of clothes being worn, and eaves drop on the conversations around me. I was very embarrassed when I saw the men's costumes, and wondered at their poor taste in wearing anything so revealing – especially in public.

There were so many things that I didn't understand since coming to this country, and even more so since being away from the confines of school. I spent my time observing everything and everyone, while I tried to stay invisible and safe.

Parents & Promises

Once again I had to travel alone on the bus, for high school resumed long before college. Arriving back at school in the evening hours, I was allowed to stay the night at the Thompson home and go back to the dorm the next day. I was glad to have one more night before coming face to face with the one person on campus I dreaded to see.

That night, when I was in bed, Aunt Betty came and talked to me and what she started to say scared me silly. The woman who had assaulted me had been expelled, and someone had mentioned my name in the investigation. Had that woman hurt me? Now I was in a spot, for once again I did not wish to lie as I knew it was wrong, but if I said anything - well, the Wangkai in me just knew she'd hunt me down and kill me for sure. I settled for saying that I knew who she was, that she scared me and had grabbed me several times. I added that I was fine - well I was in a way - because now she was gone from school, but I secretly worried lest she lived nearby and would yet "get me" as she had promised.

Fear of being attacked again had me constantly checking over my shoulders to see who was walking behind or near me. I was always tense and nervous, and even more so when in a small-enclosed area with only one other person present.

My childhood training in the bush, with all of the instincts for survival, returned as I began once again to rely heavily on my senses to keep me safe. From the day I was molested I began a new survival technique, which I carried out each time I entered a room. I always looked for escape routes, locating all the doors and windows, as well as possible spots in which to hide quickly should the need suddenly arise.

My parents seemed to have been gone forever, no one seemed to understand or care what happened to me, my stomach seemed to be in a knot most of the time, and I sometimes wondered if I was going to lose my mind to my paralyzing fears.

In school we learned another Bible verse, which was like a promise from God to me, that He really did care about me. We had the King James Version of the Bible, and it read like this "And the peace of God, which passeth all understanding, shall keep your hearts and minds through Christ Jesus." Philippians 4:7. Some days I quoted this verse in my mind at least twenty-five times, and each time I told God that He promised to keep my mind so He had better do it, because I often thought I just could not face another day. Then we learned another verse which was located in 2 Timothy 1:7 and said, "For God hath not given us the spirit of fear; but of power, and of love, and of a sound mind." For years these promises of God lived in my mind continually, even when I could see no change in my mental or emotional health. Each day I woke up to the same fear - where, by whom, and how I would next be attacked.

1961 arrived just as 1958, 1959, and 1960 had with no apparent change in sight for me, until one day a letter from Mum said that they would be coming back sometime this year. My excited anticipation had made the months just seem to drag along, and now the year was drawing to a close for it was November, and I still hadn't heard when they were due to arrive. I finally steeled myself against any hope of seeing them before 1962 for I knew that they had been gone from Cundeelee for five long months.

November 22 they arrived in Seattle, but it was December before they arrived in the town where I was living. While I recognized them as my parents, I found our meeting was almost like a meeting of strangers, for I was no longer the thirteen-year-old they had left behind. For over four years Stephen had grown up as an only child, while I had learned to work, trust no one, and be as independent as was possible in a boarding school with a multitude of rules and people constantly telling me what to do. I really felt the loss of family togetherness I had been dreaming we would share. I was not willing to risk sharing too much or show any emotions for fear of doing something wrong and being rejected.

For them the next two weeks were filled with visits to churches and friends while I continued to live in the dorm doing my studies and after-school gratis.

Dad and Mum had intentionally timed their trip, and our return travel by train to the USA and Seattle area in particular, so we could spend Christmas holidays together as a family. Little did we realize this would be the last Christmas our whole family would ever share together.

After the holidays were over, Darlene returned to school to complete her last four months and graduate. She was the first and only one in our immediate family to graduate from college.

After the holidays were over I was to learn about change yet again. I was now in a strange new country, which was actually where I had started life, but it was awful, for now everything British was wrong. I was halfway through the eleventh grade and all I knew was British – history, money, sayings, spelling; even the way I pronounced words used the British accents.

U.S.A.

An Outback Child, at Heart am I,
In culture and language, until I die.
Two cultures war now, inside of me,
Each one wishing, to be complete and free.
But ties to the past, bind me fast.
Differences so vast, forever will last.

Do not be anxious about anything, but in everything, by prayer and petition, with thanksgiving, present your requests to God. And the peace of God, which transcends all understanding, will guard your hearts and your minds in Christ Jesus. Philippians 4:4-7 (NIV)

Seattle & Spelling

After arriving from Canada we settled for a few months in Bellevue, Washington as guests of the Anackers. Their daughter Kathy was dating my older brother Dale.

I was still naive enough to think now that my parents had returned we would live happily ever after as a family, and this time would all return to Australia together. I continued to harbor these hopes, but unfortunately they had no substance except in my mind. I soon learned one person's reality is not someone else's. The following is a quote from a letter written by my father during Jan. of 1962. Dad writes about each one of us, starting with Darlene in Canada, Dale in the service, and then "Marilyn has settled nicely in her class at Bellevue High School." The letter continues with "her course was changed so she can graduate from school next year and she will be glad to be through." The last part was very true, but as for settling nicely, I think he forgot, or just ignored, the mornings I threw up and felt so ill, when he said, "it is just nerves" and took or sent me to school anyway. I was used to having a two to three foot isle between the boys and girls, yet the very first day at this new school I had to share a bench seat and desk with a boy because I didn't have a book. What trauma!

After four years of separation with little real communication on either side, my folks didn't know that fear ruled my life. I felt they did not stop to consider the last four years and what a "segregated" life I had lived. Now I was literally bumping into boys all day long, which was, to put it mildly, very stressful. I spent more hours dreading going to school than doing homework. I never realized the "shell" or mask I presented, in an attempt to be brave and appear to fit in, was done so well I was fooling everyone but myself.

I was born and raised in an era that taught that children were to be seen and not heard, not talk back, tattle or whine. While the above makes for the appearance of harmony in the home, an over abundance in my opinion creates its own problems. Whatever the culture a person has to learn how to talk, tease, interact in dialog, and find out what is acceptable and what is not, whether at school, play or in the home. I was a very good listener, but did not know how to respond to people, and so for emotional protection kept my own thoughts strictly to myself.

I had just started to feel a sense of accomplishment and understanding in my Canadian school, and now once again I was expected to fit right into a new and alien environment. The money was similar, but different, the expressions people were using were unfamiliar and foreign sounding. There was the spelling of certain words, and even the way letters were written, which were now incorrect and marked as spelling errors. In writing any word using the letters r, g, and q, I soon learned that they would also be considered as errors unless I remembered to use the "American" way of writing them. Words such as musick were now music, colour was now color, centre was to be spelt center, the list went on and on, and of course my pronunciation of words was all wrong as well. My grades plummeted and my self-esteem was once again in shreds for I felt as if I was starting at the very bottom of the learning scale once again. Kathy helped me to make a couple of friends in this new school but, just as I was starting to find my way around, spring break arrived and we moved yet again.

Although we only moved from Bellevue to West Seattle it meant transferring yet again mid-term. It meant starting all over again with new subjects, teachers, and classmates for the last couple of months of my eleventh grade. I had now been in three different schools during eleventh grade, and this latest school had more people in it than the whole school and town put together in Canada. I knew no one and was intimidated by the masses, lockers, and classrooms. While I could find my locker, the lock was a complete mystery to me and I couldn't figure out how to get the lock open once it was shut. I made sure the combination was left on the back so anyone could open it for me. When I arrived at school I would get someone to open it so I could put my coat away, and then carried all of my books around with me all day long. Each class had a big text book, and since this was long before backpacks, my arms and I grew weary of carrying them to and from school as well as all day long. I dreaded being told by a teacher to put my books in my locker and to only bring the ones I needed to class, and to go to my locker between classes. If I obeyed the teacher it meant that I had to either, stop and ask someone for help with the lock, or get to class late with no book. I still did not know my left from my right, let alone how to open that awful combination lock. I wished that I could just have a key for the lock like my suitcase had, but that was not an acceptable type of lock in that school. Boys running into me, teachers being so impatient with my slowness and lack of understanding, locks that would not open, and just plain fear of everyone around me made five days out of each week a living nightmare.

The next four months were rather strange at home also, for I was now the oldest child in the house and so had to learn a new role as to how I fit in the family. While I was now with my own family, the difference was they had all been together in one place for the last several years, and I had only longed to be there. The only time I learned about what had taken place at Cundeelee during the years they had been gone was when Dad had a meeting or showed slides. It was as if I was sometimes part of this family and at other times I wasn't and I still hadn't figured out how and when I was a part of it. It was funny in one sense since no one even knew I remembered any of the language, but if Dad would say a Wangatha word incorrectly, in my mind I would say it correctly and think "score one for Marilyn."

I found Seattle wasn't as cold as the snow-swept Prairies, there were a lot more trees, it rained and the sun rarely shone, but I learned I could cope with the weather as long as I had the security of being able to live with my parents.

Summer & Stuck

The spring and summer of 1962 was memorable in several ways. It was the first time in five years that just our family had lived together in the same house. Dale was still in the service and could only come home now and again, but I saw more of him that summer than I had in the five previous years. Little did we know it would be twenty-eight long years before our family would once again be reunited, albeit for only a few short days.

There were so many small, shared fragments of life with my family that summer, that I remembered and hung onto - a hoarding of good times just in case more bad times were around the corner. Dale would often come for a weekend visit bringing one or two fellows with him to work on their cars in the garage. He always came into the house to tell me whether to stay in the house (out of sight), or if it was okay to come outside while they were there. Since he was always trying to protect me I would follow his orders, knowing if he did not want me to meet a fellow, then for sure I didn't want to either, so no lemonade and cookies were dispensed by me to the garage on those days.

When we had first moved into the house we were renting for the summer months, the back yard was a mass of dried grass between two and three feet tall, and looked like a field of overripe grain waiting to be harvested. Stephen and I got the after school job of cutting it using the only tools available which were a scythe and a sickle. Both instruments were very hard to handle, not very efficient, and rather dangerous in our unskilled hands. The scythe had a long handle and was swung level to cut the stalks off about three inches above the ground. After three tries, each a near miss of my left leg, I decided to stick with the sickle. Instead of standing and bending over to cut the grass, I would sit on the ground cross-legged, grab a handful of the dead weeds and grass, and give a whack. It might not have been the right way and it was very slow going, but I felt a lot safer doing it my way. I often found that there were several ways of doing things, and that "my way" was often controversial and definitely not the norm. Eventually, one weekend, due to the fact we were taking too long to get rid of this fire hazard, Dad gave us a hand. He used the scythe very efficiently and so was able cut down the rest of the dry grass in no time at all.

This was also the summer Mum, Darlene, and I spent many hours in farmers' fields picking anything that was in season. We picked everything from beans to berries for what seemed to be a whole lot of work for very little pay. We would ride a bus to the field where we were given instructions about how and what to pick, and when we picked beans, a very large basket was supplied in which to place them. After being told which row to pick in we would pick until our basket was full, at which time we walked back down the row to the check-in area to have the basket weighed and checked to make sure we were picking only the ripe ones. When picking the berries, the day did not seem as long since the flats we filled were not nearly as large as the bean baskets, plus we were allowed to eat as we picked. I soon realized the more berries that went into the flat rather than my mouth meant more money in our family's pocket at the end of the day.

My parents really believed what the scriptures taught in the verse in Ecclesiastes which said "Whatsoever thy hand findeth to do, do it with thy might." No shirking was allowed, even if I was wet, tired, and sick of picking produce, or whatever the job entailed, for so was everyone else, but that was not an acceptable excuse to stop working.

Several values and standards stand out as having been reinforced in my mind by my parents' lives and work habits that summer. When I gave my word stick to it was one, as well as the principle that any job I said I would do, I was to do with all my energy and as well as I knew how. Another principle was to be thankful for a strong body and mind and for the physical capability to work.

For over four years, while my folks had been gone, inside of my head where no one but me entered, I had clung tenaciously to "my culture" by deliberately remembering people and events from my past at Cundeelee. I had even gone further, making it a practice to remember the language, so much so that for many words I still thought in Wangatha first and then translated them into English. I was a very lonely, shy person, who most of the time did not understand what was happening around me, so I took solace in remembering a stone age nomadic people who had welcomed me into their culture, language and families. Of course I remembered the good times of hunting for snacks, sitting telling stories in the dirt with my friends, and blocked out the camp fights with spears or whatever weapon was at hand which had resulted in much blood shed, and necessitated medical attention.

All summer long our house was sort of like grand central station with people coming and going at all hours. Some of the people wanted to talk to Dad and Mum about missionary work, others just needed to talk to someone, and then some just liked to be with "people of note." People loved to tell me how lucky I was – especially one young man. He was a cocky, good-looking, young man who loved to hang around my parents and my Dad in particular. One Sunday afternoon, I was sitting by myself on the porch when he came to visit and, instead of going inside as he usually did, he walked over and stood frowning down at me. Since I did not speak, he decided to say what he had obviously been aching to tell me for a long time. He started out softly telling me what nice parents I had, and I had no quarrel with that, for they were lovely folks. I really liked my parents and thought they were very special people. All too soon though he got to preaching and messing with things he had not a clue about. He started out by telling me I was spoiled, and proceeded to tell me I had always lived an easy life and knew nothing of hardships. I can still see him standing, legs apart, hands on hips, glaring at me and hollering as I jumped up and swiftly ran past him slamming the door behind me as I ran to my bedroom, where I spent the remainder of the afternoon.

This time, with less than two weeks left before my folks were to return to Australia, it was with heart wrenching certainty I realized I would once again be left in a foreign land and amongst strangers. This news was a devastating blow to all of my quietly harbored hopes and dreams. I still did not know "WHY" I was being left, for that was one of the things I had learned not to question, and still could not bring myself to break with "my" traditions.

Darlene desperately wanted to train as a nurse; however, due to her frailty the doctor advised against it. She decided to stay in America and train as a dental technician, so it was decided we would share a flat (room) in the house of two old maid sisters. These were the same sisters who thought Mum should be delighted to make the three of us dresses out of their very old and very well worn black cast-off jersey dresses. The sisters were beginning to make lists and tell us of the rules, which we would have to adhere to when we lived there. At this point I really didn't care where we stayed or what the rules were (we'd had tougher rules at boarding school) - I was just thrilled that I would be living with my sister. There was not any open discussion among family members about what was to take place, just a statement of the fact that these were the plans for us. I must admit that in these years of "growing up," I often wished I could have one or two things changed about me, and then to my way of thinking, maybe my life would be easier. The first thing I would have liked to have been able to change was my sex, for surely no one would attack a boy. The second desire came from a longing to be with my parents and friends and live at Cundeelee. If I had been born an Aborigine then I could have stayed at Cundeelee and been with my folks. Sometimes homesickness and self-pity seemed to overwhelm me and I made life even more miserable by allowing these thoughts to grip my mind, sometimes for days on end.

Less than a week before my folks were once again to be on their way to foreign shores, the cold wind of a sudden new and drastic change, blew through with yet another new challenge left for me to deal with - on my own.

Edstroms & Excursions

For the first time in years I had a wonderful sense of security about my future. I was not happy about staying in America, but had resigned myself to the inevitable, deciding to be happy that at least I would be living with a loving older sister. What I did not realize was my folks were not entirely happy about where we were going to stay. They were looking at it in regard to years, while I thought I would return to Australia when I had finished high school the following year. Not realizing my situation had once again been mentioned in church, I was both unaware and unprepared for a sudden shift in plans.

A family with a girl a year younger, but in the same grade as I, and a son five years older, told my folks they would be willing to take me in and treat me as one of their family. With only two days until we were to move into the flat, I was told that instead of living in peaceful seclusion with my sister, I would be living with a family as of yet quite unknown to me. Totally shocked with what I heard left me speechless, numb and full of dismay. What had I done that I was not allowed to live with my sister and must instead live with another new unknown family!

Why could I never live with any members of my own family - why was I always the one to be "given" away, to try and fit in with other people's family. Other people's children seemed to get to stay with their own family and I never could. It was not fair; it simply was not fair, but then when had anything in my life been what I could call fair. There were so many times that I desperately wanted to cry, holler, scream in frustration, but knew from past experience that it would do me no good. Instead I thought of all of the Wangatha words that weren't, but could be made to sound like swear words, and angrily shouted them over and over in the privacy of my mind. Over the years this habit helped to reinforce many Wangatha words and phrases that I otherwise may have forgotten. This was my only safety valve since I felt that I had to stay on my best behavior all of the time. I certainly didn't know what I would do if this new family decided to kick me out. My parents had no phone, and would be once again living ten thousand miles away, so it was with dread and fear I geared myself for the challenge ahead of me.

I have no recollection of when or how my parents left, or even if I saw them off or not, but I do remember the first night in my new home.

All of my senses, especially my eyes and ears, were on full alert to try to do everything right because I was once again in a new and alien environment. I heard Mrs. Edstrom tell Linda to ask me if I liked sweet potatoes, and when Linda asked me I shook my head and whispered "no." Now she wanted to see what this invader of her territory would do, and relayed the message "it's okay."

When we sat down to eat we bowed our heads, which was normal for the way I'd been brought up, to thank the Lord for the food. The words that I heard, which later I learned were in Swedish, came as a total shock. They all spoke together and I had no idea what was going on or what was expected of me. When it was quiet I opened my eyes only to stare in disbelief at my plate, for there sat the largest sweet potato I had ever seen. A quick glance at each person's plate around the table brought me to the conclusion that I definitely had the very largest one of all. Across the table Linda was watching me with knowing laughter in her eyes concerning my predicament, but miracle of miracles there sat a stack of bread on the table. Three pieces of very well buttered bread, and everything else on my plate, helped push the sweet potato down my throat almost untasted. I declined Mrs. Edstrom's gracious offer of a second helping of sweet potatoes, before risking a quick glance at Linda's dancing eyes.

That night I stayed awake a long time reviewing past events in my life and trying to figure out how best to deal with my new situation. Finally, exhausted in mind and body, I went to sleep without coming to any conclusions. I was just very happy knowing tomorrow was Saturday and I could sleep in if I wished. I awoke with a start. I was lying on my stomach, sensed a strange bed and room, but worse I could not move my legs. Luckily my years of being an outback child taught me to lay very still until I assessed the situation. Moving my head until I could take in Linda and her bed, I saw she had quite a large radio on her legs, and after turning even more I saw that I did too. No one in the family would ever admit to playing this prank on us.

It was several months of suppers before Linda bailed me out one evening saying "Mom, Marilyn hates sweet potatoes" and her

Mom said in shock – "and you let me give her the biggest one her first night here!" So went the life of this foster child trying to fit in and appear to cope in new and uncharted alien waters.

Life was not all fear and dread, for once again, although lacking in understanding concerning my background, this family accepted me and tried to make me feel at home. They loved to get the car out and take drives on weekends and on Sunday night after church. This opened up a whole world of sights; sounds and places that I never realized existed. The view of city lights from the top of a hill gave me a small idea of just how many people were packed into this city called Seattle. The sound of lapping waves as we strolled down at Alki Point when we got a Sunday evening ice cream treat reminded me that God was in control of the universe. What I enjoyed the most was the few times we took a longer drive to a picnic near a stream, for the peace and serenity of the woods calmed my tensions.

I'll not forget the Saturday morning I tried to open the screen door to go out and down the front steps and couldn't since something was blocking the door. I stopped pushing to ease my body though the opening and grasp the parcel that was in the way. I brought it in and laid it on the table – never checking the label since I'd never had a parcel. I figured it was a mail order purchase for one of the family, and did not want to be considered nosy checking something that was none of my business. (In each place I stayed it was always a fine line in my mind as to what they considered to be right or wrong. I had no wish to do something wrong and make trouble for myself.) As I turned to leave, Linda said "It is for you – Look your name is on it." I looked at it in surprise and sure enough there was just my name in big letters on the brown paper with no postmark or return address. As I glanced at Linda she said "Don't look at me, I didn't put it there! Open it." It was a large rectangular box, and as I opened it I saw white tissue paper then blue corduroy material. It turned out to be a lovely matching jacket and skirt that fit me perfectly. There was no name telling me who the seamstress and giver was and for years I never knew, but they could see I loved it for I wore it until it was thread bare. As a result of not knowing who had given me such a lovely gift, I tried to treat everyone the same, for I didn't know if the person I might ignore could in reality be my benefactor.

Since I didn't know what I wanted to do with my life, and had no verbal skills, I took a test at school to see what aptitude I had towards any future job. I actually scored the best in mechanics, while the second was in people or community service skills, but was told since I was a girl I had better forget mechanics and go into some type of social work.

Now they had determined what field I would probably go into, it was decided I would not have to make up math, chemistry, science, or a foreign language – all of which I had missed. Instead I was to take such things as English literature and composition, speech, bookkeeping, and four history classes to learn about the state of Washington and the USA. There were also two programs I was signed up to work in, which were to help the lady in the school library, and to work as a candy striper in the hospital.

Now, in the Edstrom home, we sat down to the evening meal as a family, with conversation about the day, and happenings for tomorrow being discussed openly by all. I had learned that when someone was talking, the others listened and then the subject was open for discussion. Now in watching and listening, I had come to the conclusion that their son Pete just loved to pick apart or pounce on any word or conflicting idea that was aired. At first he scared me because of his constant sarcasm and wit; however, it was not long before I realized he was unwittingly teaching me, by example, how to use my tongue as a tool or a weapon. It was after several months of living in their home and listening to Pete and Linda, that the inevitable happened, which was a retort to one of Pete's comments. I am not sure who was more surprised, Pete or I, but not willing to pass up a chance at a crack, Pete replied "aren't we sharp tonight" to which I replied "as a tack." When there was silence after my remark, I realized with a small spurt of surprise, mixed with pleasure, that I was learning a very valuable skill, which I began to sharpen as the months passed. I learned how to sidetrack a person questioning me by pouncing on a word or phrase they'd used, thereby diverting their attention away from me, and back to themselves.

With access to the library, I started bringing books home to read on the weekend. Once my chores and homework were done, and especially if it was a rainy day with the fire going, I loved to sit curled up in a chair and read the afternoon away. It was a time when I could and would block out everything around me, and become so totally lost in the book that it would take several tries for someone's voice to penetrate my concentration. I always picked out books about people, animals, places, and ones that looked like they would have a happy ending, even peeking sometimes to make sure, for I had experienced enough violence. In this way I was able to relax, unwind a bit, and totally escape into another world, before having to return with a bump back to reality.

School was a very busy, terribly confusing, often frightening and definitely lonely place for this very shy timid girl with her strange background and ways.

Stephen & Speech

Once again I was in what I called a survival mode, where I was totally focused on only what was happening to me as I tried to figure out what I had to accept, versus what little I could control. With some of these variables figured out, I would try to hide my insecurities, and usually appeared to all around to be coping very well in my new environment.

I had no one to talk to that understood or even cared about my background, fears, or thoughts. When I would read in the Psalms about how God knew all about me before I was even born, and that He loved me, I was comforted, but still often wondered why I had been born, as each year seemed to be more of a struggle emotionally.

For years I never knew where my sister stayed during this time. I knew she was living somewhere in the area, because I would see her from time to time. I understood about not seeing Dale, since he was in the military; however, I never understood about not spending time with my younger brother.

It was weeks before I even knew my younger brother, Stephen, had also been left, and was living in a home only six blocks away from me. Twice I went over to visit him, but was told my visits upset him, and I was discouraged from going to see or visit with him for months at a time. I could understand what he was going through, but I could not visit him, and so it appeared to him, would not visit with him. Dale's infrequent visits were tolerated.

In those days, parents or adults over us made many a decision without imparting to us any of their concerns or information as to what was taking place. We were often left bewildered and struggling to understand how to deal best with the realities brought about from their decision. While we knew and understood a little about Dad and Mum's commitment to God, and love for the Aborigines, and knew they were doing what they thought was best for us to get a good education, it did not lessen the pain of separation or the feeling of being abandoned.

As a foster child I felt the need to obey, never question, always be on the alert for any hint of disharmony and hope that I had not caused it. It was as if I walked around on tiptoe, never allowing my feet to become firmly planted, since I knew my situation was not permanent. There was no feeling of security in my life when I lived with these nice families, for to me this was just another stopping place before I was home in Australia. I always tried very hard to fit in as best I could and do what was expected of me. Sometimes this very action caused the Mom in the house to make such statements as "I wish you would be more like Marilyn." Oh how I hated to hear those words, for comparisons of foster to natural children only caused division, hurt and strife.

While I admired Linda for all of the skills she appeared to have in coping with her school work, fitting in socially, and knowledge about society around us, I was often puzzled at her stubbornness and how far she would carry it. Maybe I was jealous for I had never been allowed the luxury of making a decision for myself. By now, I was like a sheep, for I could follow well, but had no idea at all how to think or act for myself.

We were both taking bookkeeping, and while Linda was excelling, I was close to failing. One evening we sat on our beds until nearly midnight as she tried to help me grasp the idea of credit and debit. Why couldn't they just say plus or minus, rather than credit (no credit cards in those days) and debit - words that were spelt so similarly that I continually mixed them up in my thinking.

At the end of the semester, it was only thanks to Linda's unfailing help that I passed bookkeeping, and now speech class loomed in front of us. I could not believe my ears; in order to get a passing grade, we were expected to get up individually, in front of the whole class, four different times in one semester, and give a talk. Oh, how I dreaded the day it would be my turn to stand up there, for I was not even bold enough to talk to the students around me. From living with other families to living in a dorm, I had been used to following rules and obeying, regardless of what I wanted to do, and so the idea of not getting up and talking never entered my head as a solution. One by one, the students got up and told about their family, vacation, or friends. I suddenly thought "I'll talk about the only thing I really knew about and they didn't," - the Australian Aborigines. At the end of each speech the class was allowed to ask questions, and then the teacher would "constructively criticize" the topic, order of information, and the way it was presented. The embarrassment, sweaty palms, and very nervous stomach were all present, as were my notes, when my day arrived to speak. The teacher called my name, and I slowly walked to the front of the class wondering how do I start. It was then that the thought hit me to pretend to be "Karlkurla" (wild pear) the "free spirit" and not scared Marilyn. As I stood facing the class I said "Ngayuku Ini Karlkurla" and with that I found I had their attention, and switched to English. At the conclusion of the speech, and after answering all of the students' questions it was the teacher's turn. Her favorite comments were always about pronouncing words, opening one's mouth, and clarity in speech, besides structure and so forth. Mercifully, all I remembered was that it came as a complete surprise to hear the teacher's voice saying, "I have never seen someone who could talk so plainly when she barely moved her mouth. But still work on opening your mouth." That day when I went home, I was totally exhausted, feeling drained and totally worn out from the stress of the day. I shuddered when I thought about standing in front of the class three more times.

Linda had often said that when it came her turn, she would not get up in front of the class to speak and would take her grade based on the tests we took. I thought she was just joking, for everyone knew we had to obey the teachers and do what they told us to do regardless of our own feelings. We had been placed in different speech classes, and so it was only after my sweating it out twice in front of the speech class, I learned she had been serious. The third time I talked about Australia, even though each talk was a different topic and slant, the teacher told me to get a new topic for my fourth speech. At the end of the school year I passed speech class, but then so did stubborn Linda, in spite of her lack of speeches in class. True to form, my life experiences even in school seemed not fair, for the teacher had said if we didn't speak in front of class we would not pass the class, and I had believed it.

A fellow in my speech class wrote for the school paper and was always looking for something or someone to write about. After my first talk he decided I would be an interesting subject. After talking to me, he wrote a nice little piece in the school paper, which made me a curiosity for a few days, but in the end it just showed the kids how different I was and the barriers stayed in place.

College & Caring

I am sure you have heard the rhyme, school is over, oh what fun, lessons finished, play begun. I had hoped, now that I was finished with high school, I would be going back to Australia. I received no letter to tell me they would welcome my return, but rather they wrote asking what college I was planning to attend. Darlene had returned to Australia around July/August of 1963, and Stephen had also been welcomed back, but not me.

I was not a good student, and not interested in any more schooling, but dutifully filled out applications to two schools, and after including copies of my grades mailed them with little interest or hope. Surprise, surprise, I got accepted by both, and now came the choice of where to go. Up until now I had always been told when to come and go, where I was going to stay, and now I had a decision to make on my own and I didn't know what to do. No one sat down and talked to me about how to make this decision, the cost or how I was going to pay my way or anything else, for I was now considered to be a grown up.

The Canadian school was actually cheaper, but I was tired of cold weather and was also afraid the woman who had attacked me would find me for sure if I returned. I did pray about it, as I often did about things, but in the end what made up my mind for me was as simple as, Linda was going to one of them, and at least I would know someone if I attended the same one. In my bewilderment and uncertainty over my future, a touch of security in my insecure life was often all I ever tried to find.

Once again I packed my two suitcases, which were still able to house all my worldly possessions, and set off with Linda and her folks to San Francisco and another new school, which now was referred to as College. To me it was just another new and still scary environment called school.

I was nineteen, almost 5'3", 85 pounds, and wanting to be obligated "to no one for nothing." We arrived at the college grounds, and as Linda's Dad (Father Ed as I call him), unloaded the suitcases from the trunk of the car, some of the male students came down the college steps to lend a helping hand. I had already picked up my two suitcases and started on my way, when a fellow stopped in front of me saying he would carry them for me. Not realizing he was being polite I took it as an insult that he thought I was not able to do something he could. As I looked over my shoulder I saw girls handing the smallest of suitcases to the men to carry for them. I thought how phony they were, for they were certainly strong enough to carry their own things. I told him the other girls seemed to need help, but that I certainly didn't, and with shoulders straight walked on up the stairs, not allowing either suitcase to appear to be the least bit heavy.

Once again it was policy to be assigned roommates and not pick our own. Linda's roommate was from Arizona and mine was from Thailand – yet another missionary "kid." Now, Linda's folks were the closest thing to parents I had around and I desperately wanted things to stay pretty much the same – some semblance of security. When Linda's folks met her roommate's parents it was like long lost friends meeting. While I could not begrudge them such a lovely friendship, I felt a real blow once again that others all seemed to have families and loving relationships and I was on my own with neither kith nor kin nearby. I felt it almost like a slap in the face and my hard core, don't care, attitude was sorely tried. I was so very envious of all the family groups milling around me. Everywhere people were laughing, talking, hugging and smiling.

After checking around it appeared to me that I, alone, was all by myself.

When I registered I was assigned a person to help me figure out the classes I needed to take, and then passed on to a person to talk to me about how I planned to pay for my schooling. How naïve can one be? I was so dumb I had no idea of tuition costs or how this all had to be paid for - by me. There were job openings in businesses around the area, and I was given the address of a restaurant needing a worker. I still do not know why the job I got was so far away from the school. I had to take a bus, another bus or a jitney, a cable car and then walk two blocks in order to reach my assigned destination. I worked most evenings, and weekends, often traveling when buses were packed tight with humanity. With such closeness, many felt free to fondle or stroke my anatomy on the sly. I tried to get as close to the front of the bus and the driver as possible, wear a long heavy coat, and when possible sit down. Even these precautions were sometimes inadequate against a bold opportunist. I remember one night in particular when I kept moving until I finally got a seat right near the bus driver. The fellow I was trying to get away from continued to follow me, trying to slip his hand up under my coat and feel my thighs. I changed seats, I stood, I smacked his hand, I told him to leave me alone, and finally the bus driver told him to leave me alone and he did. This twice a day, hour to hour-and-a-half trip, six days a week, kept my stomach in knots and my nerves feeling raw and vibrating in tension.

I eventually became acquainted with some of my classmates working as night watchmen, and between ten and eleven at night they were usually waiting to let me in, for the doors were already locked. Each night, when I stepped off the bus, I ran as fast as I could towards the school hoping the night watchman would be waiting. Sometimes I was in fear of my life as I ran, for I was being chased by unknown young men, who had been on the same bus, and gotten off at the same time I had. This was the situation I had landed in, and so tried to cope with the situation by myself, in the best way I knew how, for it never dawned on me to get help by telling someone my problems. I only knew to try and stay alive one day at a time.

Here I was, nineteen, in college, and had never learned to think of what I wanted to do or be, and certainly not form any of my own opinions. The professors, especially in my English, Bible, and Psychology classes, were saying they wanted me to express my views, my thoughts, and my ideas, both orally and on paper!

During my years in the Outback I had learned well to watch, wait, and copy, but I had never learned to dream, plan, or think for myself. The years I spent in Canada I had been overwhelmed just trying to exist in a new culture and language, and try to catch up to my classmates. I had no lessons in thinking. Imitating people, memorizing everything, obeying all the school rules, and following orders of what to do and when, left little room for creative thinking. The only things I remember thinking about during these years was my survival, getting back to Australia, and not shaming my parents in any way. After coming to the USA it was first my parents, and then the Edstroms that I had tried to please – not by consciously thinking and planning, but with the unspoken motive that, if I was good enough, maybe this time I would get to return to Australia.

I, who had been so programmed the last five years to respond with the correct behavior when told how, what, and when to do something, was at a loss as to how to respond. What did they mean, what did I think? Didn't they realize that it had never mattered to anyone what I thought – and now I didn't know how to even start thinking for myself. It was exceedingly painful to realize I needed to put logical ideas, thought out by me, down on paper. I had no ideas, reasons, or thoughts. Especially worrisome to me was how to form the right conclusions – the ones the teacher wanted. My head began to ache as I realized the enormity of the new challenge I was facing.

For a while, I was so stressed out I couldn't even hear the teacher's voice for the pounding going on in my head. Amongst the sea of students, I sat frozen with the fear of failure being magnified and playing over and over in my mind's eye. I knew in my present state I was panicking, and so quietly (with my eyes open) started praying in my mind. I just told Jesus that He knew where I was, and why I was there, even if I didn't, and that I did not have the slightest idea where to begin to solve the unfamiliar and new idea of thinking for myself. As I sat, overwhelmed and despairing, it suddenly dawned on me that I did have a skill and had used it well in the past. I had the skill of listening when people talked, and observing other's reactions to them. I had always lived by other's ideas or wants, so the first part was easy, but the next part took time for me to figure out since I had no close friends in whom to confide or discuss my dilemma. It took me a long time to realize that if I listened well in class and on campus, I would know what others thought, and then could sift through what I had heard and thus decide what I liked or didn't like and why. The only thing I worried over now was whether or not the teacher would like or accept "my ideas." It was quite a while before it dawned on me that my prayer had been answered, even if it wasn't the way I thought at the time was best for me. I would have dearly loved to forget about school entirely.

Because of my high school aptitude test results, I was assigned to major in Psychology. I didn't know what the word meant, nor could I at first spell it, but the class turned out to be a blessing in disguise. In the next two years I took general, child, then adolescent psychology, and with each class I learned more about how this culture "thought," and in so doing, I learned about how to exist in it. When I wasn't studying or working, I could often be found sitting, in the patio-like area in front of the school, just listening to students talking. By the second year, many of the men students realized I would listen endlessly to their tales of woe about their girlfriends and, if they asked me, I would tell them how to "fix" their relationships. I had watched most of them together so often that I could usually tell them when and what had gone wrong. At first a few of the women got a little huffy with me, thinking I was after their man. When they got their man back, and he was willing to work on their relationship, then all was forgiven.

Trying desperately to blend in and at least appear "normal" I went out on a couple of dates. It wasn't long until I learned I had been invited out due to a challenge, and that I was more of a challenge than a delight. After a year of traveling on city buses to and from work, I was becoming even more nervous and paranoid than when I had arrived in San Francisco.

Emotionally I could not cope with a fellow by himself, but several times I went out with a group of students. As long as I was not expected to eat anything, and no one touched me, I was okay, but if a male student grabbed my hand I immediately and without thought, reacted by throwing up. It was so embarrassing. If the group went to eat after our outing, they knew I would be a cheap date for I couldn't even drink water, and I had to be on an outside seat. Before I ever sat down, I quickly scanned the area, finding and memorizing where all of the exits were, as well as the location of the rest rooms. I could help others with some of their problems, but I could not handle my own daily nightmares.

My college days taught me much about the world I now lived in, from people with different life styles, to the pros and cons of unions in the work place. I also learned a lot about myself, and no longer wanting to be a captive to my consuming fears, knew I had to start dealing with my problems, in tiny steps, each day.

In June of 1964 my brother Dale and his girl friend, Kathy Anacker, were getting married, and wished me to be there; however, I just couldn't come up with the hundred dollars for airfare. Kathy's folks just couldn't see me being so close, and yet not be able to share a special time in my brother's life. They sent me a ticket, so now I not only had to figure out how to get to the airport, I also had to face my fear of flying. The wedding was lovely; the plane trip quite bumpy.

Linda's roommate Jeanine invited me to "fly" home with her for the Christmas holidays. I was able to get a couple of days off from work and with churning stomach and much dread once again boarded a plane. The McGee family made me feel right at home. Little did I know how many times our lives would touch in the future or how very precious to me this family would become.

Underneath my facade of a hard shell I still had a very caring heart, especially for anyone I perceived to be an "underdog." The restaurant in which I worked was buffet style. The customer told us what they wanted; we dished it up and handed it to them. I had noticed that every day, around the same time, when the rush was over and there was a lull, an older man came in by himself. He picked up a tray and then very slowly pushed it down the rails while gazing at the food. He never spoke, but instead pointed to whatever he wished to have. One day the puzzle over his not speaking was solved when a co-worker said to me, "here comes the deaf man," as he walked in the door.

The few short blocks I walked during my trek to work, people were always trying to hand me literature of some kind or other. A few days earlier I had actually accepted a piece of paper, which turned out to be the alphabet in sign language. For about a week I studied and tried to master the hand contortions until one day, when this man stood in front of me, I signed "HI" to him. I had never seen him smile or change his facial expression, but that day his face lit up, as his eyes began to sparkle, his lips parted in a huge grin, and oh, my, how his hands started to talk. For the rest of the time I worked there, when he came through the door he came straight to me, and we slowly worked our way down the counter with him grinning and slowly signing what he wanted.

I was struggling with faith and trusting God for myself during these dark days when danger seemed to lurk around every corner. It felt as if every waking moment I was fighting fear in my mind – sometimes just worrying, and sometimes due to my real life daily circumstances.

It was during these tough days that I began trying to focus on other people and their situations by reaching out to them, and in so doing had less time to focus on myself and my fears.

Motorola & Marriage

By August of 1965, I still had not finished paying off my spring semester tuition, so when Linda and Jeanine said "Let's go to Arizona and work for the next two years," I decided to go with them. I made an appointment to see my counselor. He thought I was ready to choose my fall classes, and instead learned I planned to leave school. He even offered to put fifty dollars of his own money towards my tuition if I would just "hang in there." I thanked him for his kindness to me, but I just could not stand to be any deeper in debt - and for what. I had not been taught to value education so to my limited way of thinking college was just the latest place to which I had been shuffled.

Linda and I arrived in Phoenix September 3rd, 1965. The temperature was well over the century mark, the sky was cloudless and blue, and I was surrounded by desert type vegetation. All these similarities gave me the feeling of almost being back in my beloved Outback.

We settled in with Jeanine and her folks, with the understanding we would immediately hunt for work and a place to stay. Linda and I both went job hunting with our specific skills in mind. Linda had worked as a bookkeeper for a radio station, and I looked for work in the food industry. I had been making $3.25 an hour in San Francisco, but learned here the top pay for the same type of job was $1.10 an hour. Neither job included benefits. We looked for two weeks, and were wondering about our move here, when we were told Motorola was hiring. We figured it was worth a try and the three of us went down to apply. We soon learned it was not as simple as filling out an application and waiting for the results. After handing in our completed forms of paperwork, we were scheduled a time to return the following day for a series of tests. The first day it was all written tests. After each test we sat and waited until they called out names, never sure if they were calling out the ones who had passed or failed. The second day the same method was followed, only now it was dexterity tests, from wooden pegs and holes to tweezers and tiny bead like things – all timed of course. We were exhausted by the end of the second day; however, all three of us were still in the "running" for a job, and told to return the next day for our final test. The final "test" was a physical by a doctor.

We were hired to work the graveyard shift at the wage of $1.78 an hour plus benefits, which included, after working a year, a week of vacation. We found an apartment, and made arrangements to carpool with two married ladies. On September 23rd, 1965, with the temperature still up around 100 degrees at midnight, and the odor of the stockyards filling the still night air, we reported to work. The first night we were given vouchers, which were only valid for that night, for a full course meal (at around 3 in the morning), and for a donut and coffee at each break. Most of us felt so "wiped out" by the time our early morning lunch rolled around, we tried to take a short nap rather than eat. During the first six weeks of working this shift, all I wanted to do was sleep, but in time my body adjusted until I could eat anything at any time of the day or night.

The first several weeks my hours at work were spent trying to manipulate tweezers with my hands encased in cotton gloves topped with a rubber fingercot on each finger. My job was to straighten TO5 leads. Each TO5 had eight, ten, or twelve gold-coated wires, about a half to an inch long, coming out of a metal cap (head) with all the leads pressed together at the other end. Unnecessary talking was prohibited so in order not to nod off with boredom I started racing with myself each night to do more than I had the night before. After several weeks I was moved to the hand testers – now they were fun. I put a unit in a socket, pressed a button, and placed the unit in whichever bin the light indicated. Soon I was moved to the switching tester where I had to read a meter (numbers rolling), switch a switch, read it again, add it to the previous readout, and check if it was within certain limits. I hated adding things, so to make sure I was doing it correctly, found a paper and pencil and was working along, when suddenly my knuckles were rapped with a ruler and my paper and pencil seized. I was told to do it in my head and quickly. I finally figured out what numbers it could be between to be okay so I only had to add the questionable or close ones.

I was still as nervous as ever, but sleeping days and working nights helped me not to worry so much about someone attacking me in the dark. Well, until there were reports of women attacking other women in the bathrooms at work. At night the halls were quite deserted, construction areas lay spookily silent, and there were few people around for they were just beginning to hire workers for the night shift. For several months we were told to always carry our sharp tweezers (we also had a rounded pair) with us, and to walk with someone we knew until they caught the women. There were only three men in our area (one foreman and two technicians), and around thirty women of all ages, backgrounds, and life styles.

In January 1966 a technician left and was quickly replaced by another, whose name was John. I memorized what he looked like, furtively monitored his actions over time as he dealt with the women, and in my head placed him in my "nice" category. I was not the tiniest bit interested in him as a person or a man, just careful, thinking only of staying safe.

The three of us girls each had a desire and were saving a little each week towards fulfillment. Linda wanted a record player, Jeanine a yellow Mustang, and I was saving towards paying my way back to Australia. We sort of shared the work around the apartment, or rather did what we did best. I mostly cleaned, for living in homes and boarding school I had never learned to cook.

It wasn't long before the people at work knew I had not grown up in the USA, and that I believed anyone could have a personal relationship with God by trusting in Jesus as their Savior. Some of the women made fun of me and deliberately told dirty jokes and stories in my presence. They always knew if I understood or not (mostly not) for I would turn a brilliant red in embarrassment. There were two older women, who could swear with "the best of them," but whenever I was near would caution the other women to watch their language. They also realized I hated to be surprised by anyone, and tried to let me know, if at all possible, when I seemed unaware of someone getting close to me. One night while I was struggling with adding the rolling numbers, I did not hear the new technician, John, walk behind me. He spoke and I flew out of my chair, turning it over backwards, which forced him to step back, and the next thing he or I knew was that I had my two fists about an inch from his chin. I was poised to strike, but seeing his astonished look, I settled for saying "don't ever surprise me like that again," set my chair up and went back to work. It was a long time before I stopped shaking. He found out from someone I had been raised in the Outback, and asked me some questions, which I answered quietly with no added information. It was not long before he asked me for a date, and I said "No." I could not say I did not date, for I had gone out on one date with a young man to the ice skating rink. I had worn gloves and did not eat anything. I was not going to let myself like or get serious about any man for I had been kept from Australia long enough, and I was going back.

The next week, John asked again, and this time I was ready with an answer. Linda's aunt had talked to us one day about problems arising when a person married someone other than from the same faith, as she had. Now John was an upright and good man – didn't smoke, drink, or mess around. Several women in my department at work were just wishing he would look their way, but told me it was obvious he was "stuck on me." I did not believe them for one minute. The next time John asked me out, I again said "No," and he quickly said "Why not?" Taking a deep breath I replied, "because you are not a Christian." He was astounded – he'd been to church as a youngster and was a good person. I was not talking about church, religion, or works, but belief, a free gift, forgiveness and eternal life – not my ideas, but from the Holy Scriptures. He wanted to talk further so I eventually relented enough to let him drive me home, saying we could talk as he drove. He wanted to stop for something to eat, so I said "go ahead, but do not order anything for me." He was hungry after working eight hours, driving me home to 7th Avenue in Phoenix, and still had to drive all the way back to his home in Apache Junction. He ate I did not.

One weekend in May, the three of us girls drove over to Disneyland. The Sunday we were gone, John drove over to our church in Phoenix, and attended the morning service. A week later he again asked me for a date, and I gave him my standard, pat, and happy "NO." Once again he asked me why not, adding if it was because he was not a Christian, well, he now was one, so there. All I could think of was "Think fast, Marilyn, it has to be a trick." Out loud I said, "Are you willing to talk to our Pastor?" They talked for three hours, and when I got my Pastor by himself I asked him what he thought, and he said, "After talking to John, I feel he understood the decision he made, and now really is a believer." To my thinking this was great news in regards to John's future after death, but I was now in a quandary as to how to not go out on a date with him. My problems started with extreme fear, shame of not being able to eat or hide my extreme nervousness, and I was beginning to like him very much, yet had no intention of doing anything but return to Australia. I had heard about girls who led fellows on and I did not want to do that, so I figured I would go out once, thus showing him what a disaster I was and then he would leave me alone. He was quite a bit older than me, had never been married, had a great sense humor, and full of sharp witty one liners. This man from Montana was almost as tenacious in some respects as I was in others. He started driving me home two or three times a week, often stopping off at Bob's Big Boy drive-in on Central to get "us" something to eat. In time I learned that a sip of just plain water would not stay down, but a tiny sip of vanilla crème coke would. He would sort of ignore me while talking, and eating, trying to get me to relax and take a bite. I hated being embarrassed and scared to even try a bite of food or a sip of my drink in his presence. I was so tired of daily battling with my nervous stomach, and making a spectacle of myself. Many days I wished he would just leave me alone to wallow in my sorry state. At times it looked so inviting to just give up the fight, rather than continue to face months of enduring one step forward and two steps backwards. I had prayed often for healing, hoping for an instant miracle, for I did not enjoy the effort involved in facing my fears and the constant struggle to win even a tiny victory. I think that the Creator of Heaven and Earth has a terrific sense of humor – just look at the variety of animals He made and the creative ways in which He provides us with the help we need. I wanted instant success, but He saw the real need of my heart. I definitely did not consider John as an answer to my prayers, but rather like a pest that would not stop bugging me. I knew it had taken years to mold me into the chronically fearful person I had become, and only dimly did I remember the Aborigines with untreated wounds took a lot longer to heal than when the wound had immediate care. Cleaning their wounds was painful, but a must before the wound could be treated with medicine, and healing could begin. My mind was like a festering, untreated sore of fear which, although it started in my past, was now threatening to destroy my future.

From 1957 on, life for me seemed to be colored in black or white, right and wrong, but I had never considered myself as "religious." To me, religious meant pious, conspicuous, proud, making sure everyone knew about your good deeds, and looking down your nose at others. So it took me by surprise when John took me to meet his folks to be greeted by his dad (Pop O.) with "so this is the religious girl." When I got back to the apartment that day Linda and Jeanine asked me where I had been and I told them about meeting John's folks. They rolled their eyes, laughed and said, "well we know what that means don't we!" For years I had been meeting people, mostly older, and it hadn't meant anything, so why were they making such a fuss? They finally stopped teasing me long enough to explain the custom of "showing off an intended to the family for approval." Seeing the horrified look on my face, before I stomped out of the room, had them once again wiping their eyes as a result of their uncontrollable laughter.

I was not amused.

Jeanine passed her driving test and upon receiving her license bought her dream car, but neither Linda nor I had a license. I had taken driver's education in my senior high year, but had only driven an automatic, and her car was a stick shift. John had been trying to get me to drive his 1965 Corvair, which was a stick, all to no avail. One day, on our way home, he took a detour down a dirt road, and pulled off onto the shoulder where he turned off the key and sat looking at me. Suddenly he said, "Kiss me, or drive." I thought he was joking, but looking at his face as he leaned towards me made me move like lightening. It was hardly complimentary, but I was out of the car and standing by the driver's door before he could lean any closer. I ground the gears and bunny hopped at first as I fumed about his actions, but soon the car and the road had my undivided attention. When he did eventually kiss me I felt my world tilt with the magic of it, and knew I would soon have to make a decision between John and Australia. This decision did not come fast or easy, in fact it was agonizingly painful. It meant giving up a fantasy I had lived with for ten years, and putting my future and trust in the hands of a man. I had been heard in the past to say, "I would never wear gloves or a hat to church" (for I considered them "sissy"), always loftily adding "neither will I ever get married." In college I had been required to do the first two, and now I was toying with the idea of breaking my last voiced "never." I had longed to belong to someone for so long and now here was someone who claimed to love me, but what of my dream of returning to my "home in the Outback?" I finally stopped to consider that my folks no longer lived in the "Outback" of Australia, but on the coast so where really was home for me? It finally dawned on me that the choice of where I would live was all and only mine to make.

I really did not want to say "no," and yet I was terrified to say "yes" for I was still almost paranoid in my fear of men. I believed in "for better or worse, till death do us part," but I wondered how long he would, if he married me. He warned me, a couple of weeks before he "popped the question," that he was going to ask me a certain question only once, so I had better have my answer ready.

I was twenty-two and had only been to two weddings, neither of which I had been privy to any of the planning. Once again, Mrs. McGee clued me in about protocol for a wedding, from ordering flowers, and a cake, to photos, music and attendants.

My brother Dale and wife Kathy came down from Seattle, and as my only relative in attendance, I asked him to give me away. Father Ed and Hazel Edstrom arrived, and after meeting John told me "they approved of my young man."

We were married in the spring of 1967.

Birth & Burial

The first years of married life were filled with surprises, shocks, fun, work and a variety of learning experiences. I had never learned to cook, but fortunately John knew enough to keep us from starving. During the second week of married life, while John was at school, I got out the recipe book, which had been a wedding present, and decided to try my hand at a tuna casserole. I peeked at it right before he came in the door and it looked fine. He took one step inside, sniffed, stood still and said, "I hate tuna-fish" – nor would he eat a single bite of it. In the past, sulking, hysterics, or poor me, had never been allowed, and I definitely was not going to cry and show weakness - so now it became my choice as to how I dealt with this first mini crisis. I realized I didn't know what he would or would not eat, so in order not to make this mistake again asked him to tell me what he did not like to eat. I had made many mistakes in my life, but one thing I tried extremely hard to do was to never make the same mistake twice.

Life continued to be very busy, for we worked six and sometimes seven days a week, plus we were building a home. In the fall of 1967, we had contracted to have a home built by a valley builder, but the last snafu of putting on a rock roof instead of shingles was one too many. John and Pop had built several homes in their past, so we decided to buy a lot and build our own home. Coming from Montana, they were used to basements, but valley builders said the walls would crack and basements were not practical down here. John and Pop had the basement dug and cinder block laid, and then it was time for me to lend a helping hand. Off and on for the next week we stood in the trench between the bank of dirt and the blocks brushing on tar, then plastic and then tar once again. It was dirty, sticky, tiring work, especially after already working a full shift. We finally got the outer shell of the house done then moved into the basement with our appliances - a refrigerator and a two-burner hot plate. We lived in the basement for the next two years during which time we worked almost daily to finish up the inside. Since I was so good at copying what I had seen someone do, my husband and father-in-law would show me how to do something and then leave me to do it.

Every married couple has their ups and downs, for they come from different parents, backgrounds, traditions, and of course a different perspective being female and male. Now into this mix you add the ingredient of being a child of missionary parents, or an M.K., as we are often labeled. I have known many M.K.'s and most of us seem to struggle in the area of "things." Almost all of us have grown up in a different country, living amongst the poor. We have rarely had many material goods so we tend to either hoard things or give them (many times indiscriminately) away much to the dismay and increasing resentment of our spouse. I had been taught to give away – what was mine was yours – if your need appeared greater – even if it meant I would have to work many hours to replace it. To me this was just part of life, but to my spouse this did not make any sense at all. This was one area in which I had to learn to discuss what I thought was a good idea before I acted on my own. I had been looking out for myself for a long time by now and had these habits ingrained in me for over twenty years, so it was hard to accept there could be a different outlook on life than always sharing everything I had with others. My husband needed to learn from me how to share, and I needed to learn discernment, when to share, from him.

As part of the hiring rhetoric, all the ladies had been told that if we were to become pregnant we were to go to the nurse immediately and report when the doctor said we were due. The nurse would then set our termination date to coincide with the start of the sixth month. The women at work kept a sharp eye on my figure for the first six months, and when my physical appearance did not change, alternated between caustic comments and advice.

We had been married for more than three years when I started throwing up all of the time. Over the years I had heard various pregnant women talking about their doctors, and so now chose the one of whom I had heard only positive things. He told me to try several things to avoid throwing up, one of which was eating crackers and drinking seven-up before rising - nothing worked. I had started out working in the final test area, been moved to the probe area after our marriage, and then later to a quality control lab. I was so fortunate to be working in a lab when I became pregnant for it was a miserable five months of keeping a trash bin right next to me.

Daughter number three in the McGee family, (June) lent me two of her (three times used) maternity outfits, and with a top and bottom I bought myself, my wardrobe was complete. Still stuck in my "old culture's ways" I did not ask any questions and no one volunteered any information. In 1971, almost to the day of our fourth anniversary, I was given a baby shower and my walking papers at work.

John's folks, especially Pop, was thrilled over the prospect of an heir for John. Mom O. was a very quiet person and I seldom knew what she was thinking, but from her actions I knew she had accepted me for who I was and was happy for us. I was now home alone at night, fearfully awakening to every unexpected sound or kick from a very active baby. I had the baby crib up and pretty much everything was ready and waiting for our longed for bundle of joy. We had discussed names we both liked, and had narrowed the list down to about six. I finally stopped throwing up, although cooking hamburger made me extremely nauseous.

I was in the seventh month when one Wednesday morning I suddenly woke up realizing that my very active baby had let me sleep all night. As I started thinking about it, I couldn't remember being kicked since late the previous afternoon. Around eleven the same morning I called the doctor's office, and said I needed to see the doctor NOW and explained why I thought I should not wait until Friday morning. The nurse came back on the line to tell me the doctor said babies sometimes like to rest, and not to worry, and I told her something was really wrong, but she said come in on Friday.

I did not know about going to emergency at a hospital, or getting a second opinion, and with no close friend to talk to I decided to obey the authority figure of the doctor. Friday came and there still had been no movement, and in my heart I knew the worst had happened. The doctor and nurse came in breezing a cheery hello, saying that new mothers just worry a lot, and let's just first check the baby's heart beat. After checking several times in different places he said very quietly, "I guess we had better have a sonogram" – it was my first. I could tell from the way the doctor was clenching his jaw and the formerly cheery nurse was now oh so silent that the results were not good. No one would look at me. The doctor said "we are going to give you a shot today, and another on Saturday to try and induce labor, and if you haven't had the baby by Monday morning, we will admit you into the hospital." A flicker of hope remained since no one told me that the baby was dead. Monday I was admitted into the hospital, but it wasn't until Tuesday that I delivered, by natural birth, a baby girl. The delivery nurses spoke in whispers, and the doctor only arrived just as the baby was born. I never saw her for she was immediately whisked away. The doctor quickly disappeared also, but I could hear him talking to John in the hall. Little Miss Big Ears heard John ask how I was doing and the doctor replied "oh, she is handling this just fine." I wanted to throw something, for I was not handling this just fine - I was very, very upset. Why did he keep talking to John and not to me or at least to both of us? He went on to tell John he needed to go to a funeral home and make arrangements to bury the baby for any baby over three pounds had to be buried. Mrs. McGee arrived and asked to see the baby and was told she couldn't, but she could see me after a little while.

Once again, settled in my room, the doctor arrived to ask if I had any questions regarding the baby. I wanted to know why she had died and if she had any hair – later I thought of a zillion other questions, but it was too late. She had died because the cord was wrapped three times around her neck, and she had a lot of black hair. I named our baby April Rose. It was not a name we had discussed or mentioned, but to me it was what "her" name should be.

Dear, helpful, Mrs. McGee once again entered my life; this time to take me home with her for a day while John tended to things they thought I knew nothing about.

I called my family overseas, and brother in the states, telling them our sad news, but the hardest to inform was John's folks and in particular, Pop. It was a face to face meeting and once again I was "guilty" of not measuring up, of failing, of not fitting the "norm." My fragile, slow-growing, self-confidence was badly bruised. Shortly after this, Mom O. took me aside one day and told me John had been a twin. They had both been around three pounds, and even though the baby girl had not lived more than a few hours, Mom had always called her Dorothea. In later years, I was to learn few of the family members knew she had ever existed. John had been a "surprise" arriving eighteen years and one day after the first child and twelve years after the last baby. He was so tiny; his first bed was a shoe box. Since he was fighting for his life, all focus was on him and not the dead baby; however, Mothers do not forget them.

John and I sat down one day, soon after our devastating loss, to discuss our opinions, thoughts and choices. I had experienced many losses of one kind or another, but I must confess this was almost too much to bear. We saw that our decision now would affect the rest of our lives. We could choose to become angry, bitter, and resentful, or we could choose to accept what had happened, love each other, and try to enjoy life by taking it one day at a time.

Although John said he loved me, I was deathly afraid I really was a jinx and this would be too much even for him to bear. I just waited for the day he would walk, for others who said they loved me had left and I had never figured out what I had done to be left, time and again, with different people. I was immature, insecure, and afraid to love my husband too much for fear of losing him. It took me years to realize he really and truly had meant it when he had said the words "for better or worse, till death do us part." To begin with there were a lot of "for worse" times, but as he hung in there and we grew to be friends as well as lovers, learning to depend and trust each other it turned into "for better" in regard to our relationship to each other.

Starting with losing "April Rose" in the spring of 1971, we would next lose a nephew, and then in 1972 Mom O. passed away and I felt once again the shredding of my heart over her loss. Six months before her death she had been in the hospital and our pastor had visited her. At her funeral we learned that on his visit they talked of eternity, and she had prayed asking Jesus to come into her heart.

During this year I landed in the hospital myself with a work related injury to my back. I lost all feeling in my legs for several weeks, was in traction for ten days in order to stop the unrelenting back spasms, and put on medication. I was sent home with some muscle relaxants, and told to rest flat on my back as much as possible. What I didn't know was that medicine could do strange things to the mind. I, who had never once thought of suicide, but only of survival, one day told my husband he ought to take me out and shoot me. Within a day we decided it must be the medicine, and started quickly cutting the dosage. In two days I stopped the prescription pills, went to good old aspirin to cope with the pain, and shortly regained my love of and for life, but with a permanently bad back.

I think it was mainly because I needed a change of pace, but also in order for John to meet the rest of my family that we decided to take a trip to Australia. Even though Pop was 87 he decided that he did not want to be left behind, but would like to go along as well. It wasn't as if we were "going bush," for my folks now lived in the big city of Brisbane on the East Coast. It would not really be like going home, but I would get to have a little time with my family. It had been twelve years since I had seen my folks, my sister had married and now had four children, and my younger brother had a steady girlfriend.

I chose to fly with Qantas airlines due to their unblemished record. In order to keep their record intact we stayed a few extra hours in Hawaii due to mechanical difficulties then flew on to Fiji. We had planned for only a two-day lay over, and wanted to see as much as possible, so set out about an hour after arriving on a seventy-mile tour by car over rough roads. John and Pop had slept the hours away in the sky while I had been trying to hold up the plane with prayer and positive thoughts. The driver, John, and Pop kept up a steady stream of talk, while I, being on the ground once again, could finally relax. The road consisted of one pothole after another, which kept us bouncing up and down and not gently either, so the men were astonished to see me sound asleep. They could not understand how I could sleep with my head continually hitting against the seat, and not when I was in an airplane.

We traveled on to New Zealand to spend almost a week with my sister and her family. We had a great time, but the cold, damp weather took its toll on John, and by the time we arrived in Brisbane, he had pneumonia. Thanks to a visit with Dad's doctor, a shot and some pills, John was soon on the mend. Dad and Mum enjoyed showing us "their town" including parks, a bird sanctuary and of course the shops. I was not used to seeing emu, dingo, and the proud red kangaroo in enclosed areas, but I was proud to show off these strange looking animals to John and Pop. There was one emu in the park that was an expert at picking wallets out of men's back pockets, and John and Stephen both narrowly avoided being victims.

We were just beginning to get reacquainted and comfortable with each other, when it was time to fly back home. Pop was in a stew saying he was sure we would never get back to the USA in his life time, for a strike of the radar technicians was imminent. We had to be on standby to fly to Sydney at any time of the day or night and actually ended up staying an extra two days. When we were finally in the Sydney airport, watching the disastrous readout of canceled flights, Pop started talking to the people behind us. They were from New Zealand and knew my sister and brother-in-law – what a small world. Our flight ended up being the very last one to take off from that airport for the next six weeks.

We did our original journey in reverse - New Zealand, Fiji and Hawaii, but just to touch down, refuel, and be off again. Since Fiji is naturally almost bug free, they had made a law that all incoming planes have all of the passengers disembark, the plane sealed and fumigated, and then the passengers could returned to their plane. When we landed it was hot and muggy, the temperature was in the high eighties, and it was pouring rain. We got soaked getting off and back on the plane for there was no shelter and not enough umbrellas to go around.

We were once again flying high, quite uncomfortable in our steaming clothes; the "No Smoking" sign had just been turned off, when we smelled acrid smoke. At first I did not realize it was coming from the man sitting right in front of me, for I, along with everyone else in the vicinity, was too busy coughing. People around us were muttering between coughs, but so far no action had been taken. Suddenly, much to my surprise, my quiet husband, John, stood up and leaning over the back of the seat in front of me tapped the man lightly on the shoulder. In a very calm, but loud voice, John said, "Sir, we were fumigated in Fiji, and I don't think you need to do it again" and sat down. The dirty looks and muttering around us instantly changed into laughter, as the man hurriedly stubbed out his cigar, then departed towards the lounge area.

For the rest of the trip, John's handling of the situation with wit and laughter rather than "fist-a-cuffs" was mentioned again and again with thanks.

Life and Longings

Thanks to a caring husband, over the years I progressed from walking the daily narrow ledge of uncontrollable fear, bordering on a complete nervous breakdown, to a wary calm. I no longer had a nervous twitch when tense, and could eat in mixed company. The nightmares only returned for a brief time after a bad scare, and after being called for jury duty – involving a rape. I now realized I would always live with a certain amount of fear, which would keep me checking out elevators and rooms before entering, and men before they got too close.

My life continued to be made up mostly of work, a few play times, no children, and increasing care of Pop, but I had never forgotten "my home," and my desire remained strong to return to the Outback of Western Australia and my people. An outcome of taking Pop O. overseas was his accepting Jesus as his Savior two years later – at the age of 89! Pop had been so impressed with my Dad, brother-in-law (both "Bob's") and the love showered on him by so many Christians overseas that when he came home he got a large print Bible and started reading it.

Over the years, as "sure" adoptions failed at almost the last minute, and fertility pills did not cause fertility, we had to continue to renew our commitment to not become bitter. Some days were very tough as reminders of what I did not have were deliberately brought to everyone's attention. It was hard to go to baby showers, for many were not the least bit sensitive to my hidden wounds. I constantly ran the gauntlet of being asked if I didn't have children due to my dislike of them, or was it because I wanted a career rather than children, to asking if it was due to a certain medical problem. I had "friends" place their baby in my lap saying, "here, have mine for a while." Each Sunday as I worked with the little children at church I would think, "this is what my daughter should be doing." Finally, deciding to do something positive and change my focus, I quit working with the children, plus we started going camping in the mountains every Mother and Fathers day. I did not need constant reminders to tell me I was a failure and a misfit in this society. This escape back to nature became a time of healing, for it was a peaceful, quiet place away from the noisy city, people and their expectations.

John and I were still working the night shift (graveyard) and funnily enough I was now working with all kinds of equipment. My mechanical ability was being used after all. I worked in a quality control test lab (for semiconductors) making setups using generators, meters, power supplies, scopes and such like equipment. Setting up a test required using procedures written by programmers and engineers to manually test the finished devices using pre-built fixtures such as boards and metal boxes. At night there were no technicians in my department, so we either figured out how to make it work, waited until morning and asked the programmer, or sometimes at break I'd run down and show it to John and ask his advice.

One day, I heard that the man who built our test fixtures was leaving. My husband had heard me grouse over the years about how hard it was to insert and remove a device from a test socket, for the connectors, leads, and switches on the fixtures were located in no set pattern – just all over, and in a different place on each fixture. When I told John the "construction tech" was leaving, his immediate response was "why don't you ask for the job?" "Me, ask?" I had never asked for anything, still rarely said anything more than was needed for a conversation (except to John), and thought it was an outrageous thing for him to suggest. During the next couple of days I thought a lot about his suggestion. What hit me first was John's absolute faith in my ability, and next that someone needed to make life easier for us workers. Why not me? After mulling it over, I decided to talk to my boss about letting me try out for the job. I jotted down a few notes to keep me presenting facts, not feelings (for I had learned men just want the facts), as well as the advantages to having me do the job on 3rd shift.

The person leaving had a grade 31 rating, and was only required to build and repair hardware for testing devices. Not only was I given a three-month trial basis to do the same job, but I was also given the added requirements of assisting the eleven women in our area on 3rd shift. The job now included deciphering data taken from devices tested on automated equipment as well as lash-ups, troubleshooting problems, and building and repairing hardware. It was an awesome challenge. Due to my God-given natural talent, a whole lot of tenacity, John's help in teaching me how to read schematics, some classes, and an enormous amount of hard work, at the end of the trial period, I had the job.

I went from operator's pay and hours (6 1/2 hours and paid for 8 on the graveyard shift) to a grade rating of 24 technician, which meant I now had to work 8 hours. I figured it out once that during this time I made a dollar less an hour than the women who called me for help to solve their problems.

For many years it was a constant daily battle proving my dedication to excellence to programmers and engineers alike. For a long time I just signed my initials on a completed project, having learned once they saw my work, and then learned I was a "female," they were much more likely to have me work on future projects for them without fussing. I loved my job and it suited me perfectly. I could help people, be responsible only for my own work, listen intently, and did not have to talk very much. Before this job, I had been over five women, and had never known how to deal with one real slacker who often refused to work on certain product lines. But, regardless of what job I had, each time I received my paycheck I would look at it in awe as I remembered how at age thirteen I could barely read or write. To me it has always seemed totally amazing.

My husband and I lived by the same philosophy, which was our own work came first, but if someone from another department came to us for help, and we could help them, we did. One night I did a favor for a department without a technician, for they were having trouble with a swap block, and had to have certain devices tested by eight in the morning in order to qualify for a contract. I never thought much about having built them a new swap block, or that I had gone over and checked out the data before they began testing. The next night I did check to see if they had beaten the clock and they had by a half-hour. It was a couple of months later, when I was given the "Award of Excellence" plaque that my boss found out what I had done, or I learned my "favor" had secured for the company a million-dollar contract.

I had finally done something right!

At 94, Pop was walking or riding his ten-speed bike about two miles a day on the dirt road near his home. He wanted to remain in his own home, so each time we checked on him, we would take him fresh and frozen meals. He decided to have cataract surgery that year, and it was not only unsuccessful, it was the beginning of his down hill slide, for his eye became badly infected.

Our tri-level home had no bedroom on the main floor so we turned our living room into "Pop's" room. Anyone who has had total care for an elderly, once-active, now disabled relative can understand the daily ups and downs we now faced. Pop had never been one to say "Please" or "Thank You," but as he was now living in my home I expected, and received after some tussles, these plus other small courtesies. Six weeks before Pop died, my husband John said to me "I've got this gut feeling that Pop is going to die on my birthday – not my sister's, one day before mine, since I put him in a nursing home for the last two plus months of his life." John and his dad had a strange sort of chemistry. I lost track of the times during the fifteen years we had been married, that John would pick up the phone to dial, and then just start talking, for Pop was already on the line. It happened time after time, to both of them, at any hour of the day with nary a ring being heard. Definitely weird! Sure enough, around noon on John's birthday, Pop passed away. Later that day we were surprised to receive a phone call from the mortuary requesting we verify Pop's age, for he appeared to them to be in his 70's, instead of almost 96.

Once again, Mrs. McGee and family came to my rescue. I was so "out-of-it" that I had not even thought about everyone coming to my home after the funeral, and had nothing prepared. The morning of the funeral that dear lady called from Phoenix to ask me if I minded them bringing something over. They brought everything from meat and rolls to salad, and every bit of it was needed. It wasn't until later that I learned they had called the church we were attending, and since we had not been in Sunday school for almost a year, (due to caring for Pop) they declined to do anything for us. Now I had a real dilemma on my hands or rather in my mind. Once again "Christians" had failed to meet my needs, and I had a choice to make in regards to my attitude towards them. I needed time to sit and reflect, for I felt the "slight to us" could fast become a festering sore because I did not want to forgive them. Long ago I had realized Christians were not perfect, they were just normal human beings, and as such made the same type of "people" mistakes as people who did not call themselves Christians. I needed God's help to forgive those who had no idea of the devastation they had almost wrought in me. What a tussle I had, for I wished to hold a grudge, and yet the Holy Spirit brought to mind what the Bible said in Ephesians 4:32. "Be ye kind one to another, tenderhearted, forgiving one another, even as God for Christ's sake hath forgiven you." Ouch - what a standard – the sinless God/Man Jesus died so I could be forgiven of my sins, and I would not forgive a slight. It was not easy, but for my own mental and spiritual health decided to choose joy and to think of the blessing bestowed on us by the McGee family rather than on the fact that I had been snubbed by people in my own church. It was during this time that I wrote the following poem.

I revel in the morning Lord, when birds are chirping and gay,
The sun is bright; the breeze does blow, the trees lightly sway -
My chin is high, my face aglow, my soul humbly prays,
Forgive them Lord, again I say, said, but not meant yesterday.
My feelings were hurt, by thy children Lord, once again, day after day.
I am a rose, a bud or full blown, the choice is up to me –
Forgive and move on by your strength dear Lord, or shrivel and as them be.
A bud stays tight in its own little world, closed from the noise and strife –
It stays so pretty and decorative, but misses fully sharing in life.
The kiss of the wind through each petal so soft, the scorching of the sun –
Gentle rain soothing the dirt away, busy bees having such fun -
The choice is up to me, my fragrance to give free.
Sniffed, cut, arranged, dried oh, so enjoyed – my petals won't stay neat.
I give my heart to you dear Lord, to keep my fragrance sweet.

It seemed as if we had no sooner buried Pop than we received a letter from my folks saying Dad planned on retiring at the end of the year, and they were thinking seriously of moving back for good to the USA. They went on to say they would like to live near me, they only had a very small pension and to ask what was the cost of living like, and what did I think about it? For instance, was I planning on moving any time soon?

Other than two tiny blips in time, they had been in Australia for thirty-three years. I had grown up without them, and now they wanted to be near me. Dad had already had several heart attacks;

we had just ended caring for Pop and were very tired – all these thoughts and more churned in my head. John and I talked about the fact that the small house John and Pop had built now belonged to us and was still sitting vacant – Pop had needed to know he still had a home. In the next several days we talked and prayed a lot about our decision, knowing it would cost us in energy, money and time. Before a month was up, we wrote telling them they could have "Pop's" house rent-free if they decided this was where they really wished to live out their retirement years.

Over the next days and weeks I wavered from being content with our decision to struggling with the prospect of my parents being so close after all of these years. They were virtual strangers to their own daughter. I felt guilty over not being happier over the possibility of their return. I was exhausted from caring for Pop, grieving over his death, and dealing with problems that occurred with his estate and the cleaning out of his house. We had only just begun to think of finally having time for ourselves and what a joy that would be, and now it appeared we once again might soon be called upon to at least be readily available to elderly relatives. I wondered why we were the ones to always end up looking after old folks, and never the pleasure of little ones. I had to constantly check myself lest I start thinking too much of "poor me," which I found was a subtle first step down the road to bitterness.

We finished cleaning out "Pop's" house and waited for a letter from my folks telling us of their decision.

In the fall of 1982 we received the letter from Mum and Dad saying that they would accept our offer of housing, and would be arriving early in 1983.

The day after our sixteenth wedding anniversary, and not quite a year after Pop's death, my parents arrived.

Before leaving for America they had hopped a bus and traveled across the country for one last visit with the Aborigines and my brother in Western Australia. It had been a very hot summer down under, and the long trip was taken in less than ideal conditions. During the trip Dad had a small stroke, wasn't able to get to a doctor for treatment, (and later when he was recovering his speech and help was available), instead decided to just push on.

By the time they arrived in Arizona they were on the verge of absolute collapse. The next two years were spent leaning on, and learning from us. Dad, who had loved to talk to people, now was in the process of rebuilding his speech as well as his confidence, and for quite a time wished only to stay at home and away from people. Mom could no longer hop a bus and go shopping downtown – it was walk or go in the car with Dad or Marilyn, for she had never learned to drive. Dad had to become confident enough to drive again, and on the opposite side of the road. They were once again in "their own" country, but everything was foreign to them – from money and medical coverage, to apparel, food and the way people approached life. While they wanted to take up where they had left off, since I was their long "lost" child, I was torn between trying to be the daughter they expected me to be, and at the same time be true to myself.

Return & Release

During the next six years we progressed from strangers to friends then to family trying to reap what future we could without addressing the hurts of the past. My parents were lovely people and I needed to see them for who they were and not who I had wanted them to be for the past twenty-five years. As Dad's health returned, he regained his outgoing personality, and started becoming involved in church activities and ministering to people around him. Dad was soon teaching an adult Sunday school class, and Mum was kept busy entertaining missionaries and visitors. Dad never met a stranger – they were always just someone he hadn't known before. Oh my, how he delighted in telling them a story, only to turn it into a question of where they were going to spend eternity, and on what premise did they base their reasons.

I had tried to encourage my folks to attend a church near their home, but they wanted to go to the same one John and I did, regardless of the added distance. I had only just begun to have a small sense of self-confidence, volunteer at church, and actually talk to people. What had happened in Australia and Canada once again took place, only now it was in the church I had attended for years. I was once again being referred to as the daughter of Bob Stewart instead of by my own name.

I became so overwhelmed by what I thought I was not that I once again melted back behind the shadow of Dad's charismatic personality.

Slowly over the years, and mostly due to my work environment, I had started to talk. At first it was only to stick up for the "under dog" and then, finally, for myself as well. Having been silent for so many years, I sort of became a motor mouth, and only now am in the process of learning the wisdom in "a time to speak, and a time to keep silent." There is a saying - "silence is golden;" however, being metal, gold will melt when it becomes hot enough. Sometimes it is such a small thing that triggers words to flow like hot lava, spewing forth, never to be corralled again, and such was the situation in which I found myself. One minute I was happily driving my Mum to her destination (church), when a phrase she had said to me many times in the last couple of years, suddenly became once too many. I didn't realize I was angry that people assumed, and yes, very often told me, how "easy my life had been," when they hadn't a clue at all of what my life had been like.

My mouth opened and out poured, on my poor unsuspecting Mum's head, years of pent-up anger and past hurts. I remember with startling clarity, beginning with the words, "Easy – you think my life has been easy, well, let me tell you a few facts about my so "easy" life." I started with just the highlights and no graphic details, beginning with being raped and continuing on for the next ten minutes until I was almost shouting. In my brain I wanted to continue on, and ask why they had so often written of housing young adults, yet had never invited me to come and live with them, but my heart said it was long past time to shut up.

I had taken note of the sudden stillness and tensing of my mother a few seconds after I had begun ranting, yet had continued to rage on, and now we both sat silent. When Mum at last started to speak, I quickly realized she had only heard the very first part of my diatribe, before her mind had shut me out to travel back in time. The first words out of her mouth were, "I should have known, for your panties were bloodied."

I can only remember a very few names of white men who had visited the mission during my years there; however, when Mum asked who, and I said his name, her shudder and statement "oh, that awful, awful, man" confirmed my story.

My folks had grown up with "the past, is the past and no talking will change it," so other than my mum saying "Please, don't tell your Father, for it would kill him," our discussion was over. I had no intention of ever telling my Dad, for he was dealing with problems of his own – diabetes. Mum had learned just because her daughter hadn't complained, didn't mean she hadn't encountered problems, and she never again referred to my "easy life."

For years I had coped with what is referred to as "female problems," and as the years went by, the problems only increased in severity. My doctor sent me to a specialist, who after running tests and checking me out, set up an appointment to see my husband and myself in his office. He talked to us about surgery, the risks involved, gave us pamphlets to read and told us to go home and talk it over and return for further discussion if we decided to go ahead with it. Before we left his office, my husband asked him to tell us honestly, if it were your wife, what would you do?" He said "I don't want to influence your decision, but if it were my wife I would encourage her to get a complete hysterectomy." The next several weeks were filled with paperwork, getting a leave approved, giving blood – just in case it was needed, and more paperwork. The week before the surgery I had to go to the hospital itself and fill out three more forms, the last of which was "Organ Donor." After reading it over, but just before signing it and checking "Yes," I turned to my husband and the lady giving me the forms to say, "Just make sure I am really dead before you let them take any of my organs."

I was nervous about the surgery (though not as nervous as when flying), and so with my husband's and Pastor's prayers lingering in the air, went confidently into surgery and under the surgeon's knife. How civilized it was this time, for I was out of it before I could see anything scary.

Even though I was really groggy, and couldn't seem to open my, oh, so heavy eyelids, "little miss big ears" was listening to what everyone was saying. The doctor had stood by my bed and told my husband that I had come through just fine. John had stayed for a few minutes and then gone out while relatives visited me, then they stood out in the hall talking and after a while a "nurse" came in to "check" on me. I was foggily drifting in and out of "sleep" only to suddenly perk up my ears in alarm. Surely I had not heard what I thought I had heard, which was "would you sign this form for donating your organs!" I thought "it must a bad dream" so did not answer. The voice came again – this time accompanied by a touch on my arm. Warning bells rang in my head – I must be in a lot worse condition than the doctor had said, but I needed my organs to live and live I was determined to do. A forceful "no" came out of my mouth, and I refused to sign the paper even after she asked me once more would I reconsider "NO" was all she heard from me. The next day when the doctor visited and, told me I was doing fine, I told him about the previous day's encounter and that it had made me think I was going to die. To say he was livid was to put it mildly.

I worked really hard to get out of the hospital and home just as soon as I could. The HMO we were with said we could have a visiting nurse, but John and I were used to looking after one another so I declined. The first evening home the surgeon himself called to make sure I was doing okay, and see if I had any questions. We were really impressed!

I did find out the "rest of the story" as to the reason I was approached after surgery. My paperwork had been lost; so someone had been sent down to get my signature in order for all of the paperwork in my file to be complete.

The summer of 1989 we started hearing rumors (janitors always seem to know before the bosses) that our company was going to offer a severance package to their employees. At first we didn't think too much about it, for John still had two years, and I more years than I wanted to count, before retirement could be an option – or so we thought. When the "package" was announced we listened intently to the who's, what's, when, and how, finally deciding it didn't include us. For the last eight years we had worked for the same boss, still on night shift, one cubical away from each other doing somewhat the same jobs. John is an inventor so his job (Engineering Analyst) included designing as well as writing programs for new product on five different types of machines. I had finally made it to a grade 29 technician and mostly rewrote or updated programs for four different machines, and sometimes still built hardware. We were a good team, John and I, for he could figure things out and I could do the building or the "hand work." As things turned out we were eligible to "walk," and our boss was most understanding to let us both go out together. Nov. 17, 1989 after a lovely parting party, which was attended by people from three different shifts, we walked out the door for good. John had put in twenty-six years, and I twenty-four.

I was sort of thinking of trips we could take and things we hadn't had much time for would now come to pass, but life keeps on happening and responsibility once again knocked at our door. The first week of January began with my Dad in a hospital 45 minutes away from my home, which meant I had to go pick up Mum and spend the day at the hospital instead of "playing." From the hospital it was to a nursing home for about a week, and then back home. If I had still been working I would not have been able to keep up with the demands that were placed on my time and energy, nor the emotional strength that was required during the next six, seemingly endless months.

In February, I notified my sister and brothers that if they wished to see Dad alive, they make arrangements to come in the next couple of months. I felt the weight of responsibility for elderly relatives once again on my shoulders, only this time there were added requirements. Mum had long wanted to move right next door to me so she could "pop" in for tea, fix my meals etc., but we had no money to buy anything. They were only six miles away from me, but with a big yard, which was now becoming an added problem. I had prayed much about a possible move for them. In the meantime, plans were made and the "kids" started arriving until we were all together again – after twenty-eight long years. During their week visit, they took turns shifting between homes so everyone got to visit privately and together – what a fun time. My sister and I started looking at mobile home parks close to me and after narrowing down our choice, brought in the "boys" to check out all the details we thought were their department. The amount needed was almost exactly what I had received in a cash settlement for "quitting" work, and so it was arranged to make the move. Just one thing – it would only be my husband and me with a small car that would be doing all of the work, for the "kids" had gone back to their lives and families. Such is life.

My Dad was in and out of the hospital with his bad heart and terribly infected feet for the next several months. It was during one of his stays, that as I was walking down the hall towards his room it was as if a voice spoke to me. Suddenly I knew beyond a shadow of a doubt that my Dad would die at home, and I and I alone would be with him at that time. This did not make me a "happy camper" for I did not wish to be so close to death, and in particular my Dad's, and for months I balked at the very thought. It was the knowledge and experience of death from my childhood that raced through my being – all of the taboos, superstitions, and the accompanying fears gripped my mind.

Mum was having trouble coping with many things, not the least of being without Dad. As a young married man, Dad had taken on most of the responsibility for the home – from writing the checks and opening the mail, to answering the telephone due to Mum's lack of hearing. Now I was about to reap the results, and so the two of us started a crash course for Mum to learn the basics.

Dad's doctor had been on "holiday" for two weeks, but had just returned to find her "favorite" patient was back in the hospital. I caught her before she went into his room and warned her of his speedy deterioration since she had last seen him. I stood in the hall listening as my Dad asked her about her vacation, and then asked her about the condition of her heart in regard to eternity. When she came out of the room she had tears in her eyes, and leaning up against the wall whispered, "I would never have recognized him if you hadn't told me." His weight had been dropping steadily as they increased dialysis treatment from once a week to now three times a week, and talked of increasing it even more. It was now time for me to talk to the doctors and get the information needed, for my Mum was not able to cope with the situation. After talking to the doctors, and realizing anew that there was nothing they could do, I told them I would present the facts to my parents and get back with them the next day.

It was so hard to always be the "strong" one, but someone had to do it, so while Mum was off getting a "cuppa" (tea) I sat down by Dad's bed and slowly began to talk. I laid out the options, which were simple - increase dialysis for the next several weeks, and die, or stop everything. If he chose the latter he could go home and have a nurse come once a day to treat his feet and monitor his pain medicine. I knew even as I told him these options, it meant I really would be alone with him at home, when he died. The doctors had told me since he hadn't eaten in more than a week, that they gave him only two days to live after he went home, but he hung in there for four.

Having worked nights for so many years I was well equipped now for the long silent night hours. I had finally made peace with God and myself over being willing to shoulder this responsibility. This particular night Dad was, by turns, quiet and then talkative, and wanting to call and talk to his kids for one last time in order to ask their forgiveness for anything he might have done that had hurt them. It was after ten and I could see Mum was totally exhausted, yet it took me several minutes to summon the courage to tell her to go to bed and that I would wake her after he was gone. I hadn't stopped to realized how much she had been dreading watching him go, until I heard the relief in her voice and her asking me if I was sure it was okay. I, for the first time, was honestly able to say, "Yes, it is okay with me."

Dad asked me to look after Mum, and we forgave each other for any past hurts, without bringing up anything in specific. He needed to be turned every twenty minutes and his back thumped. It was such a small service, yet I was the one to be allowed to minister to him in his last hours. It was a strange, yet wonderful four hours, in which Dad for the most part would lapse in and out of consciousness. Until the last fifteen minutes of his life, every ten or so minutes during his last hour of life on this earth he would suddenly raise his two emaciated stick-like arms heavenward and say urgently – "Up, Jesus, Up, and again Up, Jesus, Up." He always said it twice. The first time it happened I just about jumped out of my chair, for the fervency and tone of his voice was as if he was already in the presence of God. He sounded just like a small child standing next to their Dad asking to be picked up. It was as if I was sitting in a Holy place! Totally Awesome!

The fears I had lived with due to my past were suddenly gone in the realization that this was no longer my Dad lying here, but only his shell, for his soul – the essence of his being was right now with Jesus. Something that I had struggled and fought against for three months had suddenly turned into a time of joy and healing for me personally.

During the next several years, Mum earned my respect and love anew as I watched her try to learn new things and cope with all of the scary challenges that each new day brought into her life.

Flying & Firmament

I had never ceased to almost "crave" the reality of being able to go back "home." During the two years after my Dad's death, I had brought it up even more frequently, only to one day realize that my husband never seemed to be very enthusiastic. Duh – it only took me two years but one day I asked him when we were going to Australia and he said he'd been there, and was not really interested in going again. Bummer. I mulled this over for a week and then hit on an idea. What if I could get Linda to go with me? He thought this a splendid idea. That very evening I called Linda asking her to think about what I was going to tell her. I was heading for Australia and New Zealand the following year and John did not want to go, so I wondered if she would think about making the trip with me. This is as far as I got when my ear almost got blasted off with, "Thank John, thank John, I am going with you!"

We took a year to plan our trip, which would last for a month and include both Australia and New Zealand. I wanted to see my brother, get back "home" for a visit and then visit my sister in New Zealand, with of course a lot of sightseeing in between. The only thing I was stressed about was the flying, especially the twelve to fourteen hour stretches, but if that's what it took to get "home" then so be it. We wrote letters, made phone calls, checked out things to see and do, and finally were ready to head down under.

We met in the LA airport, at a pre-determined spot, about five hours before our flight was ready to leave – just to make sure neither one of us missed this long awaited trip. Our first stop was Cairns, and our arrival was at nine in the morning. We tried to take a nap, but after a half-hour said "we can sleep anytime" and off we went to see the sights and sign up for a trip to Green Island the next day. It was six in the evening before we "crashed" back down on our oh-so-welcome beds. Our favorite thing about this motel was the breakfast hole they would slide your breakfast tray in through. Off again – flying of course – this time to Alice Springs. Even in this small "hostel" we were treated to a refrigerator, with milk and tea fixings, along with the usual small electric pot with the safety auto-off switch. Even though I really wanted to see the sights such as the "Flying Doctor" and the "School of the Air," and paintings and carvings, by this time I could hardly concentrate on them for the excitement building within me. The red dirt, the gum trees, and seeing some Aborigines all made me feel like I could finally almost reach out and touch "home."

We flew on to Perth where we boarded the "Indian Pacific" train at one in the afternoon (took off at 1:40) headed eastward towards our destination, which was around 500 miles down the tracks. Stephen had gotten us a sleeper so we didn't have to sit up, which was lovely, but we were so "wired" it wouldn't have mattered at all. I had been quiet during the flights, for talking and clenched teeth are not really compatible. Now that I was once again close to "mother earth" and headed for "home" I started pointing out everything and chattering a mile a minute.

I had warned Linda that when we got to our destination, if she didn't see me do something – either ask or don't do it. For instance, she was not to take a photo of an Aboriginal unless I did; she was to do things quietly and slowly and think before she acted. At 3:20 in the afternoon we were served tea and cakes in our "stateroom" – such luxury!

Once it got dark we made our seats into beds and lay on top of them, looked out at the myriad of stars, and talked in hushed tones. The conductor came to make up our beds, and when he saw we had them already in place, checked our tickets to see where and when we were planning to disembark. Since it would be close to 2 AM when we would reach our destination, he told us he would check on us at 1:30 AM just in case we had fallen asleep.

At 10:30 PM our train pulled into Kalgoorlie for an hour layover so we got out and walked into the depot, and then along the platform in an effort to stretch our legs. I could hardly believe that after thirty-seven years I was finally so very close to being "home."

We told the conductor we wanted to get off at Coonana, for in talking to Stephen I had learned that Zanthus no longer was a stopping spot, and to say "Coonana." Now the conductor was not a "Happy Camper" for he knew there was nothing out there to mark the spot as to where to stop the train, for Coonana was five miles away from the railway line. How could he just drop off two American ladies in the middle of nowhere in the middle of the night – it just wasn't done. I told him that my brother would have the car headlights shining down the track, and he would be waving a torch – a message he relayed to the Engineer – via, of all things – a Motorola radio! Once we were about 150 miles east of Kalgoorlie the train started slowing, and the crackle of the Engineer's voice over the radio saying "so far nothing." The conductor was starting to give me a bad time, when suddenly he was interrupted with "okay, we see him," and the train slowed even more. We inched along for over a minute until I could look down on Stephen. Even after we had our luggage from the train, and I had hugged Stephen, the conductor was not sure he was doing the right thing, and again asked me if I was sure. Of course I was sure, for I was "home."

Linda, after a "cuppa" headed for bed in the mobile home, but I was wound up tight and so we stayed up talking for about an hour. My senses were already attuned to my surroundings, and without thought I was able to categorize the sounds I heard and instantly fall asleep. Upon awakening I went in to see how well Linda had slept, only to find out she hadn't slept at all for all of the strange noises. City noises keep me awake and she can sleep through them, but the rustling of a mouse, the screeching of the birds, the chooks, and the breeze through the leaves of the trees kept her awake, and put me to sleep. Ha! Ha!

While Linda was getting up, I went to find my brother and see some of "my people." I caught up with Stephen as he was finishing a discussion with an Aboriginal fellow as to what needed to be done that day. I had not stopped to consider what a time lapse of almost forty years does to a dialect; it had changed to some extent. As I stood quietly listening, I realized many of the words I was hearing were a mixture of the two dialects I had known as a child. When Stephen was free and as we started to walk away, I told him some of what they had been talking about, but added that I didn't know what a certain word meant.

I wish I could have taken a picture of his face, for to say the least he was astounded. I had never thought to tell my family that all these years I had been deliberately trying to remember my culture and language so when I returned it would be like coming home. Someone overheard our conversation, and it did not take very long for the information to travel that I still knew and understood their language. It wasn't long before I was once again sitting in the shade of gum trees on soft red dirt, surrounded by a group of Aborigines, listening and speaking a language I had learned as a child. I was home. The government had moved the Aborigines from Cundeelee to Coonana, which was closer to the railroad and brought in mobile homes in which they were to live. I found my emotions at war with seeing a people caught between the old and the new. Having gone to work in the "outside" world, some had forgotten their own language, while others could switch back and forth easily. As I watched one manipulate his way around a computer and answer a phone I was delighted; however, I felt as if I could feel their pain and understood their struggles all too well for I too was a misfit in society.

One day Stephen took us out to Cundeelee and as my journal states "the road is as bad as ever." On the way we checked out our old "swimming" hole, and in the process had Linda taste the water and check out the black goo at "Goddards" creek. There was not much left standing in the way of buildings, but Dale's tree that he liked to hide in was still standing and larger than I remembered. Stephen showed us one of the dry wells that Dad had dug in hopes of hitting water, and the foundations of where some of the buildings had been. As I stood looking down at "my valley" I was finally at peace, for I had made good my promise all those years ago, that I would return. I realized "home" for me was defined in the land itself and the Aboriginal people who had made my life special, and not so much the particular spot called Cundeelee. During the next several days I immersed myself in enjoying each moment for I knew I would have to hoard them for a long time to come. Seeing friends of my youth, and my "grandfather" (called Silly Willy due to the stories he told) talking to me a mile a minute only to be told by me to "slow down." Using the right word, but with a very funny accent that made them laugh. Stephen driving, only to stop suddenly to show us a "bob-tailed" lizard, a mountain devil, perfect kangaroo tracks, and once to go and pick a "wild pear." Memories of a time almost forgotten, were suddenly becoming real again, as we shared it with Linda. One day Stephen drove us about seventy miles to the edge of the Nullabor Plain where some of the Aborigines were camped. Linda was introduced to Billy Tea (with syrup and Sunshine powdered milk), Damper, Anthills, and sugar on tree leaves. All too soon it was time to head back to civilization and continue on our journey, but first we took our last look at a flock of Galah, some Lorikeets, and watched startled emu race away from the sound of our engine. Goodbye is never easy to say, and I must admit that this was one of the toughest ever, for it felt as if my heart was being torn out of my body. I was once again saying "goodbye" to my family, and a land that felt like home. It is hard to describe the "pull" of a certain spot on this earth, that to me feels like a magnet continually pulling at my emotions.

I was pretty true to my "culture," only allowing a few sniffles to be heard by Linda over the next couple of hours, and in less than twenty-four hours we were touching down in Wellington, New Zealand. Darlene met us at the airport and as we went to step off of the curb, I saw a car coming too close, and as I grabbed Darlene to pull her back I yelled the Wangatha word for "wait a minute." I hadn't realized I had reverted so totally that in an emergency I would not speak English. I would not have worried so much, except Linda was not watching for cars coming from a direction she was not used to and as a result was stepping off curbs, and nearly becoming a statistic.

We had a fabulous two weeks of visiting and sightseeing, but I was quietly struggling with my emotions, not the least of which was trying to always speak in English.

Pomeranians & Personalities

Joy came into our lives over the years, thanks to four fluff ball family members, who just happened to be canines.

We had been married for about a year and a half, when we decided to get a pet, namely a dog. Not knowing what kind of breed we really wished to get, but knowing we wished to have a smallish dog, we went to a pet store. We window shopped for a bit, petted a few, and were ready to leave, when a small, pure white, except for nose and eyes, bundle of fluff came racing over to me. I reached down and picked him up to prevent him from running out of the store. He immediately started sucking on my thumb, making the clerk stare, for he was known as a little terror. Needless to say "Tarzan" had found himself a home. He loved to play tug-a-war with John and a sock, and was a very curious dog. If we left anything, even a bag of chips on the table, and if every chair was not pushed tight against the table, I would find him on top of it with his nose in the food.

One day, when Tarzan was nine months old he followed John out to the mailbox. A man in a truck was going by at the time, and deliberately swerved up unto our cement driveway, hit Tarzan and drove off. When John returned with Tarzan in his arms, I figured the dog was just playing dead as he sometimes did. I had a very hard time accepting that he really was dead. All I could think of was I must really be a jinx, for John had grown up having pets and each had lived a long life, but this was my first pet.

For over a year I could hardly bear to think of getting another pet for fear of what might happen to it, but in time decided to try again. Returning to the store from which we had purchased Tarzan, we asked them to find us another white Pom.

A few weeks later they called us to tell us our Pom had arrived, and we excitedly drove down to pick him up. Out from the back came a tiny thing that could not run straight, was screeching at the top of its lungs, was orange in color, and sported a coat like kinky spiked wire. We looked at this "thing" in disbelief, while the clerk said there was no such thing as a pure white Pom. After looking at a photo of Tarzan he merely grunted. We took Tawny to our veterinarian to check over. Since he arrived without any records, Tawny was given his puppy shots. Three days later he lost every hair on his body, making him look just like a rat. Although from his looks he certainly would not have been my choice of dog, this little fellow had spunk. He eventually sported a lovely coat of hair, grew to six pounds, looked like a fox, and exhibited a caring attitude.

Now "Pop" wanted a dog, but did not want total care of one, thinking they were too old to take on such a full-time responsibility. Tawny ended up living with my in-laws from Sunday afternoon until Friday morning of each week. He always knew when it was Friday morning, and any time after 8:30 would hop up in the chair by the window to gaze down the street in anticipation of our arrival. Tawny now had two sets of standards – at "grandpa's" place bacon had to be fixed just right, for he knew if he wouldn't eat it Pop would cook more just for him. At our place he rarely got bacon, and then it was take it or leave it – and so he took it.

The three of us loved to go camping in the White Mountains, and rock hunting in deserted areas. Tawny and I would scout the area to make sure we knew our surroundings. I had been surprised to learn that while my husband was really good at finding his way around a town, if a tree got between him and his vehicle he was lost. If I was with him I'd let him walk until he was willing to admit he was lost and then lead him back, but several times I had to tell Tawny to go find John. Tawny would race off in the direction John had gone, and soon both could be seen ambling together towards camp.

Mom O. had never really taken to Tawny, but tolerated him willingly for Pop's sake, until the day Tawny literally saved her life. Mom O. had been in a car accident a year or two earlier and hit her head on the windshield. Mom O. started experiencing headaches, then small strokes, and then one day while hanging out clothes she suffered another stroke, only this time she fell to the ground where she lay unconscious. Pop was working in the garage and out of sight, but Tawny tracked him down and went into a barking frenzy, running back and forth until Pop followed him to where Mom O. lay.

Once she returned from the hospital, Mom O. spent most of her days sitting in her recliner chair. Tawny would sit up straight and tall by her chair for hours at a time, ready to summon Pop if needed. Mom O. would every-so-often reach down and let her fingers touch his head. She grew to love that little guy, and he continued his care of her until she passed away. Tawny died at the age of fourteen.

We felt lost without Tawny, but it was about a year before we were ready for our next Pom. This time we decided to check out other sources than a pet store. We ended up getting an eight-month-old pedigreed show dog whose only fault was his ears were considered to be too large. Now Precious Petey knew he was royalty, and did not take instructions or admonitions without sassing you back. He was cream colored, liked to toss his head, and strut around, showing off his six pounds with perfect poise. Petey liked to wedge himself in small places. One day we glanced over at the bookcase to see Petey sitting on the bottom shelf wedged between the books holding a stamped letter between his teeth – we laughingly said he was reading his mail.

Petey had been with us for about nine months when a breeder asked us to take a look at the runt of her litter in hopes we would give him a good home. After a couple of weeks we broke down and brought home a tiny new Pom. We were told his parents weighed two and four pounds and were assured this would be a small Pom.

When Petey first met Kodiak Cubby he sniffed him all over and walked away, only to return to check on this tiny thing that had invaded his space. At first Petey allowed Cubby to eat first, but as time passed and Cubby continued to grow, it was time to play the king and put the "peasant" in his place. Until we got him, Petey had lived his whole life in a cage with five other Poms, and although he could dance on his hind legs he had not the slightest idea of how to jump. I spent hours just trying to teach him how to go up and down our stairs without him crashing or falling down them. Cubby continued to grow until he topped out at close to thirteen pounds, and with his long legs he had no trouble with a step or stairs. Petey tried hard to keep up with his brother, but his short legs, plus his lack of skill and judgment when it came to steps almost did him in. One day John, Cubby, and Petey were all in the motorhome while we were packing it for a trip. John, with Cubby at his heels, exited down the steps, but Petey, trying to keep up, just launched himself over the steps and down onto the cement. His chin hit the payment and he was out cold, doing a perfect roll with his feet sticking straight up in the air. I had just arrived on the scene and thought he was a goner for sure because blood was seeping from his mouth. I could only think of Tarzan, but Petey was lucky for all he did was just loosen all of his bottom teeth. Our other dogs had loved to play with a ball or a toy that squeaked, but Petey never would touch or play with anything I brought home for them, and he passed his disapproval on to the younger dog. They amused themselves and us with their own games, of which the favorite was how to get the other dog out of the recliner and them in it.

Traveling was a favorite "treat" for they knew they would get lots of walks in the campground. Petey and I usually walked to check out everything, and more likely everyone, while John and Cubby ran as fast as possible only to collapse back at the campsite.

One time we finished packing late in the evening, and the temperature was still around a hundred degrees. We headed for bed, but decided to check on the dogs, for while Petey liked to go to bed at about eight in the evening (only appearing bleary-eyed and cross if we made too much noise to suit his highness), Cubby had to be carried to bed. It had been about fifteen minutes since we had closed up the vehicle inside the garage, but Cubby lay sound asleep, oblivious to the heat, and ready to travel.

One day, while driving down the road, my husband said "every sound is like a tinny echo in my right ear, and I can't figure out what is being said." The annoying condition went on for months with the final theory being it had been some sort of a virus. It was so strange – for it affected only the males in our home. In the end, John and Cubby both lost over half of their hearing, while it affected Petey's heart. On his eleventh birthday he suddenly collapsed and died in John's arms.

Petey had always been the boss, with Cubby the loyal loving follower and now Cubby was alone and did not know what to do.

Tarzan had been our curious one and the only one to ever get car or altitude sick.

Tawny had been caring, and loved to play "fetch" by the hour – especially when traveling in the Van.

Petey was royalty, yet loved to "visit" people allowing anyone to pick him up, except at bedtime.

Both Tawny and Petey had visited at a nearby nursing home where they graciously allowed everyone to admire, pat, pet, and stroke them as much as they wished.

Cubby was a real hunter, very protective of us, and we called him Dr. Cub, for any cut of ours had to be inspected by him personally.

Each of our distinctly different Poms added much joy, laughter, love, and exercise into our home. They allowed me to talk to them about anything, never criticized, and usually gave me a lick of approval before departing.

Lax & Lost

It had been four and a half years since my father had passed away, and two years since Darlene's husband had been killed in a car accident. She, Mum, and I decided that it was time for Mum to go and live with Darlene and her girls in New Zealand. It took us about nine months to decide on the right time, cost, airlines, etc., and finally set the date of her departure as Thursday evening Dec.1st. We figured going a few days early would allow Mum to be well rested and ready to celebrate her birthday on the 7th. I had been of two minds whether to fly with her to Los Angeles or just make sure that should the need arise the airlines would assist her. After talking it over with the airline representative and Mum several times, I'll admit to being relieved that everyone was confident there was no reason whatsoever for me to fly with her. Although she would have to change planes, she would be flying with the same airlines and would only have to walk past two "gates" from where she would disembark to where she would check in for her overseas flight. As an added insurance, in order to make sure she would not miss her connecting flight, we had given her almost three hours between landing and taking off for New Zealand. We had a meet and assist note on her ticket with instructions to call my phone number in the unlikely event something went wrong.

Dec. 1, 1994 was a lovely calm, beautiful Thursday evening in Phoenix, Arizona when Mum boarded the plane for the first and shortest leg of her journey. I had her two large suitcases checked all of the way through to New Zealand, so all she had to carry with her was a purse and a small (11 x 14 inch) bag made of a cloth material depicting wild animals.

We left the airport confident all of the "bases" had been covered, that Mum was safely on her way and all was right with the world so to speak. For the first time in years we felt free of the load of responsibility of having to care or look out for elderly relatives. We went to bed exhausted from the emotional turmoil of the past few days, for Mum had continually changed her mind as to what she was taking or even whether she wanted to go. Friday morning arrived, and we decided to do something we had never done before; to attend a midday movie and then just kick back and do nothing for the whole weekend. (I've often wondered what would have been the rest of the story if we had decided to go camping instead.)

On entering the house at about 5:30 p.m. Friday afternoon, we saw the message light on the phone was blinking. I pressed the message button, and on hearing one of our New Zealand niece's voice, expected to hear that Mum was now with them. Instead I heard her say Mum would not be arriving in New Zealand until Monday.

The next couple of days were a blur of phone calls to family, the airlines, overseas, and to the police to try and track her down. We had people checking the airlines and customs for both New Zealand and Australia until we were sure she had never left the country.

Where could she be, and what had happened? There had been fog at the LA airport so her flight had been rerouted to Oxnard making her arrival in LA a half-hour after her scheduled flight to New Zealand had taken off. In talking with the airlines we were able to track her movements only until 8 AM Friday morning when she had checked in for her flight. They reported she seemed rather confused when she was told to return Saturday evening at 8 PM to check in for her flight. She had not been met and assisted nor had I been called. We later found that she had actually (in error) been booked on a flight both Dec. 1st and on Dec.2nd but was told not to return until Dec. 3rd.

On Saturday I had called a niece in Phoenix who worked for a TV station to see if they could help any, and she had reported she'd called some stations in LA, but they would only do something if it were a slow news day.

It wasn't until Saturday night, two hours after the last plane had left, and at the witching hour of midnight that I was finally allowed to report a missing person, and then I played tag with whether it was Phoenix or LAX police who had jurisdiction. The LAX police asked me to give them a description of what she looked like and what she had been wearing. They assured me they would tell all of their officers that night and the next morning to keep an eye out for her as well as make a thorough check of the airport.

Sunday morning, after checking in with the airlines, the LAX police, and many hotels in the area, I decided that regardless of the lack of encouragement from any of them I had to check things out for myself. I called our Pastor telling him that I, along with a friend, were headed for LAX, and ask that during the service they pray for all of us. John stayed home to man the fax and phone.

On the way over I discussed my strategy with Terry, which was to start at the gate Mum would have arrived at, and go from there to customer service, then talk to the LAX police, and even check the morgue if needed. As we approached the customer service desk, our eyes restlessly scanned the crowd around us – ever hopeful. The lady at the desk called the LAX police, and relayed a message from them to us, which was to meet them at station 53. Having once again received directions, and now headed for the lower floor, Terry checked the left side of the room while I checked the right. It was about noon on Sunday and the airport was not very busy at all. Coming down the escalator we spotted the two police officers waiting for us in the distance.

As I hurried the last few steps towards them intent on finding out any news, Terry turned her head slightly and I heard her intake of breath and a stunned, "Why, Ethel!" My body jerked to a stop; then I turned and hurried over to where my Mum stood, and hugged her tightly. I noticed the police were looking on politely, yet as if they wondered what was going on; so after asking Terry to hang on tightly to Mum, I walked the few feet to thank them for finding her.

I began to thank them for finding my Mum, only to have them interrupt me, saying all they had been told was to meet me at station 53 and did not as yet know the reason for this meeting. Since my Mum had only been a few feet from them when Terry spotted her, we had assumed they had found her. I had just started explaining to them, "This is the lady who has been missing since Friday morning – the one you were looking for" – when I was rudely interrupted by an irate young man. He had brushed past the policemen, and was now yelling down at me, "How dare you let your Mother arrive from Australia and not come to pick her up for two days!" He continued on, "Don't you know that meet and assist is only for people who are blind or in wheel chairs?"

During this fracas the two policemen had radioed – "missing lady found," but had stayed to talk to me, and now they were really curious. The irate young executive from the airlines was still frothing at the mouth – so much so that I had to take a step back as I was being spit upon. Just as I held up my hand to try and slow him down to get a word in - the news media arrived. It had been a slow news day and they had heard "woman lost for three days has been found."

While the media focused on Mum, I expounded to the three waiting men just what had taken place for the last three days – as far as I knew. The two policemen had been strangely quiet, and asked if I knew what phone numbers I had called. I showed them the numbers I had in my notebook, and they said it was the correct one for their department, but that nothing had been said at roll call about a missing woman. Mum had not been looked for at all. They gave me their card and asked me to write everything down, once I was home again, and send the report to them personally, after which they left to report back to their boss.

Terry tugged on my sleeve, asking me if I minded that my Mum was speaking so freely to the press, to which I replied I didn't care about anything as long as we knew where she was. The media now turned to me; asking where she had been all of the time? I did not know, so they asked her why she hadn't called me and her response was, "I didn't want to worry her." With that they had their story and left, while I went back to dealing with the airline representatives. Mum had lost her ticket, but still had her passport. She had her purse, but had lost her special cloth bag and half of the contents that had been in it. The two lady ticket agents were very helpful and reconstructed her ticket to New Zealand, but the young executive would only allow it to be for a one-way paperless ticket. (After she arrived in New Zealand she ended up having to pay for another round trip ticket, for they would not permit her to buy only a one-way ticket back to the USA.)

It turned out Mum had checked in every morning at 8 AM instead of at 8 PM, (yet no flags that were supposed to "fly" when she told them her name did). She had not answered any of the evening pages, because she would leave at about 4 PM and get a hotel room for the night. She had tried to call my brother in Australia, but had the wrong number, also his phone was out of order during these three days. It was only after she had called my sister in New Zealand – which had started my search – that she had she lost my sister's number. Although she had my number and I was close – she had not wished to worry me.

I am still awed by the miracles that took place during those three days. Mum was starting to have small memory lapses; however, she was able to change her money from New Zealand into American each day to eat and get a hotel. She had never before flown alone or with this airline, yet each day she was able to return to the correct place in the LAX airport – even after she had lost her ticket and there was nothing to bring her back. Mum had always flown either Qantas or Air New Zealand and so we had even been checking with them. Mum liked to strike up conversations with any and everyone, but the Lord had protected her. The last one is still the one that leaves me with goose bumps, for when we were on the escalator looking down at the policemen, we saw no one else around them. When I had hugged Mum, she had mentioned a nice man who had just been with her; yet when we spotted her there was no one close to her at all. We know people were praying in at least three different countries, and checking back, I found that it was during the time people in our church were meeting and praying, that she just "seemed to pop up out of nowhere."

After making sure Mum caught the Sunday evening flight out at 10 PM, Terry and I went to a hotel for a bit of sleep before catching our 9AM flight for home. The next morning as we were silently and somewhat sleepily pushing our bags along in the check in line, my ears suddenly picked up on what the two men behind me were relating. They were saying "Can you believe it – that woman was lost in LAX for three days, and was found and okay!" Not having watched any TV the night before, I missed seeing my one minute of "glory" (for the media had told our story). I waited until they were all done relating how it was a lesson to them, for both their parents were beginning to have memory lapses. As I turned to say, "Do you want to hear the rest of the story," they started saying, "It was you" and, "What happened?" I wasn't hard to spot, for I was still wearing the same distinctive shirt they'd seen me in on TV. The next several minutes were spent entertaining them with the amazing events that had taken place. It helped to take my mind off the scary thought of getting in an airplane for it looked like we were going to have a bumpy ride home since storm clouds were building.

It was Monday, December the 5th, when a stomach-rolling, sweating-palms, tight-jawed flyer by the name of Marilyn boarded the plane bound for Phoenix. Just after we took off the stewardess announced a drawing would take place on this flight to celebrate the first week they had been operating this new run. She continued her talk, saying it was a computer generated random drawing; and to please have your ticket ready to show her if your seat number was the winning number called. When she had announced the drawing I had immediately leaned close to Terry and whispered, "She will call my seat number."

It wasn't as if I wished to win, for I hated flying, but I knew beyond a shadow of a doubt that it was definitely going to be F12, and even had my ticket out before she ever called my seat number. When she came to give me the papers (not transferable), I asked her if it had been rigged, for this was the same airlines from which my Mum had been "lost," but she looked truly mystified by my question.

A storm front moving from California to sunny Arizona made it not only a very bumpy flight home, but to top it off we were kept in a holding pattern for about ten extra minutes before landing.

In the end, in spite of my dread of flying, I had to "pay my dues and fly" because I loved my Mum.

Blessed and Blessings

Nowadays we are familiar with the following two phrases – "an attitude of gratitude" and "practice random acts of kindness." For several years of my life I witnessed these truths being put into action each day by my parents; then I experienced it myself through the lives of people who opened their hearts and homes to me. Having received many acts of kindness from others, I wished to pass on the blessing to others and in so doing discovered for myself joy in performing all sorts of random acts of kindness.

Having been blessed in so many different ways myself, I realized the act of blessing someone could take any form and be visible or invisible to the recipient.

Permit me to share with you two very special times when I reached out to bless someone and how in turn it truly blessed and even strengthened my own faith.

My husband says I can listen to three conversations at one time, and later give him the gist of each one.

One day at church, as I sat listening to the ladies talking, I picked up on one particular mother who seemed to be extremely stressed. She was telling about a person who, on a regular basis, paid a person to come in and clean her house for her. The woman speaking said "what I wouldn't give to have someone do that for me." It was as if an inner voice said, "Marilyn, pay the cleaning lady to do it for her." I went home, struggling with myself, for I wanted to do it, but we didn't have much money ourselves and couldn't afford the fee for a whole eight hours of work. I had heard enough of the conversation to get a phone number, so called the lady who did the cleaning. I asked her if I sent her a check to cover four hours of work, and gave her the name of the person and their phone number, would she do the work and keep my identity secret? She agreed. I had been so touched with the gift of my new suit years before, that I wanted to surprise and encourage someone in like manner. To this day, the woman says one of the first things she plans on finding out when she gets to heaven is who hired the cleaning lady?

One of the ladies I worked with at Motorola had surgery and had been away from work for quite a few weeks. I had been praying for her, when I felt I needed not only to visit her, but also take her some groceries – that very day. After talking to my husband about it, I headed for the store, thinking of bread, butter, soup and vegetables. As I went up and down the isles looking for bargains, for we were on a tight budget ourselves, I kept thinking "meat," yet resisted. I thought, why should I buy stuff for someone when we rarely buy it for ourselves. I had everything but meat, yet I kept thinking about meat and resisting. At the last minute, I got out of the checkout line, almost running to the meat department to pick up some chicken and hamburger. The inner prompting had been so strong that I felt like saying out loud, "There, are you happy now?" only now I was at peace. This inner prompting to do something so specific had never before happened to me, and I must say my heart was not really overflowing with joy in sacrifice.

After calling to make sure it was okay to drop in on her, I drove over and carried the shopping bags into the house. She was still very weak, so once inside I proceeded to unload the bags one at a time, placing the items where she directed. When I had opened the refrigerator all I had seen were empty shelves. She seemed to be amazingly intent on each item I pulled from the sack, murmuring a thank you for bread, milk, margarine and so forth, but by now was on the edge of her chair. I wondered if she was okay, but continued unloading the supplies, lastly pulling out the meat. When she saw the meat, tears ran down her cheeks, and through her sobs, I heard her say, "Thank you, Jesus."

She had been to the doctor that very morning and had been told, "Today you must start eating meat." She had been very depressed, for their remaining food consisted of only a few canned foods and no meat. At the time I called, she had told no one her situation but God, for she had been praying for a miracle.

I'll never forget my struggles over buying some meat when I saw no "earthly" reason for it. Yet, due to my obedience, God allowed me the privilege to be used in answer to a desperate prayer. Through our tears we said, "Thank You Jesus," feeling awed and blessed by His Divine intervention – yes, through a human - in her time of need.

I was blessed when GOD gave me life, not that I have always thought it such a blessing to be alive.

I was blessed by my PARENTS, when they sent me away to school that I might get an education, by their daily example of love for others, and especially through their prayers.

I was blessed to have a SISTER and two BROTHERS.

I was blessed when my BROTHER saved my life, when STRANGERS gave me – a foreigner - toys, and when the ABORIGINAL people made me one of their tribe.

I was blessed with inward peace, when GOD forgave my sins and saved my soul.

I was blessed when LONG JACK held my cot, the CONDUCTOR looked after me, the DOCTOR operated – skillfully, and a FAMILY cared for me.

I was blessed when the THOMPSON and EDSTROM families opened their homes to me, and by TEACHERS who helped me to learn.

I was blessed when DOROTHY talked to me, and each time I made a new FRIEND.

I was blessed when LINDA helped me with my studies, and by an UNKNOWN PERSON, when they left me a perfect-fitting, handmade suit.

I was blessed when I met the McGEE family, and when I got a job in Arizona.

I was truly blessed when JOHN chose me to be his wife – never understanding how he could love me, but truly thankful for his steadfast, unwavering commitment to me.

I was truly blessed when nephew KEITH and niece DOROTHY came from California to give us a two-week, much needed and appreciated break from caring for Pop.

I was blessed when SHIRLEY continued to hug me, until I learned to hug in return.

I was blessed with love from each of our POMERANIANS.

I was blessed when TERRY traveled with me to LA, and when MUM "popped up" safe and sound.

I was blessed when KAT shared her computer skills with me, and when JODY, DIANE and MARIE offered to proofread this book.

As a human being with faults and failings, every so often I find that I need to go through a reality check. Am I exhibiting an attitude of gratitude; in other words, do I choose joy in spite of my circumstances? Am I practicing random acts of kindness and compassion to or for individuals who can do nothing for me in return? Do I so focus on "poor me" and what I think I am not, that I am forever doomed never to enjoy the experiences of life?

I wrote the following poem on one of those days when I was struggling over who I was not, and needed to change the direction of my focus from myself to who I was in God's sight.

Images

My world says to me "What do you do?"
"Who do you know," and "Will your looks woo?"
And down goes my heart, into my boots,
As memories of words, and taunts, and hoots,
Resurface old wounds, again in me,
Recordings and pressures of old, I see –
Of what I should do, and definitely be,
To stay "at home" or to cross "the sea."

I cannot type or file or sing –
Unqualified to "do" almost anything.
I can bake, and clean, and maybe sew –
Wipe a nose, or the garden can hoe.
Neither a doctor, lawyer, merchant or chief –
No college degree --- imagine my grief!
No names are dropped by me, or mine,
As I quietly move, through my block of time.

Jesus cares "for me," I just now read –
Cared enough to die, and rise from the dead!
He's praying, "for me," at the Father's right hand,
Plus, building a mansion, "for me," in that land!
Awesome thoughts, now revolve in my head –
LORD, may I in obedience, always be led –
Not worried by others – looks, skills or power,
Instead, remembering, I'm your "PERFECT" flower.

And so in spite of my background and still feeling to some degree "A Child of the Outback" at heart, a misfit in society, and yes, still harboring many hang-ups, the choice of how I plan to deal with my future lies with me. I can let my past continually rule my mind until it totally destroys any future I might have, or I can choose to forgive and in doing so - start on the road towards health and living.

My prayer is that in spite of what I am not, that I will daily focus on how GOD looks at me and become the person He intended me to be - one that glorifies my Creator, Savior, and Lord, by touching people's lives with encouragement and blessing.

Epilogue

On completion of my manuscript I made copies and sent them to the two families who had cared for me, and one each to my sister and brothers. I asked them to tell me of any corrections they felt were necessary and also to let me know if in any way I had misrepresented anyone or anything.

As I sat and waited for the comments to arrive from Australia, Canada, New Zealand and here in the USA I wondered about their reactions to my book and would have loved to have been a "fly on the wall" of each home.

My brother Dale, who lives in the state of Washington, came in first with some good suggestions of reconstructing some of my sentences, along with some added information that Dad was wearing his bomber jacket when the boomerang hit him.

My sister Darlene, who lives in New Zealand, corrected a couple of the dates along with the name of the ship we returned on to the USA. She immediately knew the names of the two people who had hurt me - for I had not been the only one in either case.

The two couples who had cared for me years ago were most gracious and said there was nothing written about them that they wished to change.

My brother Stephen was the last to check in for the phone lines in his area of the Australian Outback had been out for a month. He said, "I think you had a bit of selective memory when it came to the boat incident for I certainly was punished and grounded besides." He said I could leave it in the book with his blessing.

As a result of reading my book, my sister and brothers started sharing pieces of their lives with me and bits of our history I didn't know about, along with a few answers to some of my questions.

I learned the mission board had made the stipulation that during a second term of service no children over the age of thirteen were to return and live with their parents at Cundeelee.

I also learned that when Stephen had returned to Australia the second time, within a week he was shipped off to live on a farm and did not live with our parents as I had thought.

The four of us agree our parents did not "walk on water" and made some mistakes as all humans will, but overall they really were two of the most SPECIAL PEOPLE we have ever had the privilege of knowing.

THE END

Glossary

Bloke	a fellow
Billy Tea	tea brewed over a fire in a tin can
Chooks	chickens
Damper	a bread without yeast
Jumper	a sweater
Milo	a drink similar to Ovaltine
Pegs	clothespins
Primus	a camp stove
Sheila	a girl
Sleeper	a railway tie
Spinifex	clumps of spiny grass
Ta	thanks
Tilly	lantern
Torch	a flashlight
Ute	a light utility truck
Vegemite	a spread for bread
Wireless	a radio
Weetabix	a breakfast cereal

Looking at "My" Valley

Swimming Hole

Thompson Family & Marilyn

Dorothy

Edstrom Family

John & Marilyn

Tarzan

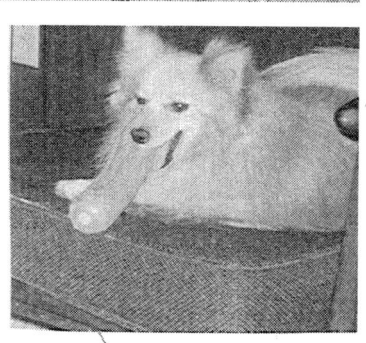
Tawny

Cubby/Petey

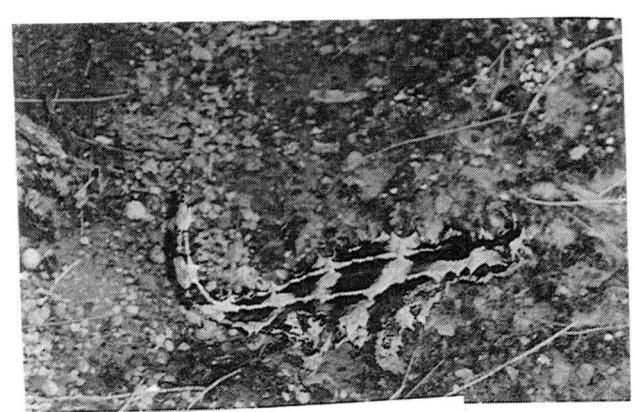

Mountain Devil

Wild Pear